tender
topics

tender
topics
picture books about
childhood challenges

DOROTHY STOLTZ, ELAINE CZARNECKI, AND BUFF KAHN

an imprint of the American Library Association

HURON STREET PRESS

CHICAGO • 2013

Published by Huron Street Press, an imprint of ALA Publishing
Printed in the United States of America
17 16 15 14 13   5 4 3 2 1

Extensive effort has gone into ensuring the reliability of the information in this book; however, the publisher makes no warranty, express or implied, with respect to the material contained herein.

ISBNs: 978-1-937589-34-9 (paper); 978-1-937589-49-3 (PDF); 978-1-937589-51-6 (Kindle); 978-1-937589-50-9 (ePub)

Library of Congress Cataloging-in-Publication Data
Stoltz, Dorothy.
    Tender topics : picture books about childhood challenges / Dorothy Stoltz, Elaine Czarnecki, and Buff Kahn.
        pages   cm
    Includes bibliographical references and index.
    ISBN 978-1-937589-34-9 (alk. paper)
    1. Picture books for children—United States—Bibliograph 2. Conduct of life—Juvenile literature—Bibliography. 3. Children—Books and reading—United States. 4. Reading—Parent participation. I. Czarnecki, Elaine M. II. Kahn, Buff. III. Title.
    Z1033.P52S78 2013
    001.62—dc23   2013005066

Book design by Kimberly Thornton in Interstate, Pauline, and Miller.
Cover photograph © Thai Soriano/Shutterstock, Inc.

♾ This paper meets the requirements of ANSI/NISO Z39.48-1992 (Permanence of Paper).

To my brother, Walt, and my sisters, Gloria and Irene,
who teach me the art of living. —*Dorothy*

To my big sister, Kathy, who taught me that books are
magical things, and my big brother, Artie, who gave
me a hero in real life. —*Elaine*

For Steve, Ian, and Alaina, with all my love. —*Buff*

Contents

Preface ix

Acknowledgments xi

Introduction xiii

Part I: Why Tender Topics?

1 | Helping Children Develop the Love of Reading   3

2 | Get Your Kids Talking   7

3 | What Makes a Good Picture Book?   11

Part II: Selections on Tender Topics

4 | Friendship   17

5 | Resiliency   25

6 | Life Lessons   33

7 | Feelings   43

8 | Curiosity and Exploring the World   57

9 | New Baby   65

10 | School Days   73

11 | Physical Illness of a Child   81

12 | Money   85

13 | Moving   91

14 | Military Families   95

15 | Adoption   101

16 | Learning Disabilities and Behavior Issues   107

17 | Diversity   111

18 | Vision, Hearing, and Mobility Issues   117

19 | Divorce   123

20 | Bullying   129

21 | Death of a Parent or Loved One   135

22 | Death of a Pet   141

23 | Mother Nature   147

24 | God, Spirituality, and Awe of Life   153

Afterword 157

Resources 159

About the Authors 165

Index 167

Preface

If I feel grumpy, what should I do?

*I want to be friends with Ben. Why doesn't
he want to be friends with me?*

*Is it okay to be proud of myself the way Toodles the Turkey learns
to be proud of her gobble-gobble in* I Want Your Moo?

Do I have to tell Grandma I ate the last *cookie?*

THE DAY WILL COME WHEN YOU WILL NEED TO HELP YOUR child confront similar or even more challenging questions. Our goal is to assist you in finding great books to share when that conversation happens. A well-chosen picture book can make a huge difference to a child trying to navigate the unknowns of life. But children can't always locate these books on their own. They depend on the adults in their lives—parents, librarians, teachers, counselors, friends, or family members—to guide them, and with thousands of picture books available, picking out the right one isn't an easy task. We created this selective guide as a tool to help you. We hope you will keep it at the ready and use it to lead you to the perfect book for your child.

Who are we? Dorothy Stoltz relishes her role (and her gobble-gobble) as an outreach and program coordinator for a public library system and cheers herself by listening to classical music. Elaine Czarnecki cherishes her work as a reading specialist and university instructor and relaxes by curling up with a good novel and her cat, Jazzy. Buff Kahn treasures her experiences assisting people of all ages as a children's department supervisor in a public library and kicking back in her flower garden. To this book we bring our professional perspectives, our love of books, and the courage to confess to eating the last cookie from time to time.

We hope the selections we have gathered will show your children how books can enlighten them as well as help them take advantage of the opportunities that life's challenges offer. We want children to see the light that shines through reading and take pride in their gobble-gobble, the way Toodles the Turkey does in Marcella Weiner and Jill Neimark's wonderful story.

Acknowledgments

E'D LIKE TO THANK THE FOLLOWING PEOPLE who have made a difference in this book: Saroj Ghoting, Paul Hammer, Kathryn Lobdell, Valerie Smirlock, Emilee Stoltz, and many other friends, librarians, teachers, and counselors who answered the call for favorite tender topics picture books. Thanks to the staff at the Westminster, Annapolis, and Eldersburg libraries for handling many reserved books for us.

A special thanks to editor Stephanie Zvirin, who gave us the opportunity to create this resource, and to educator-author Virginia Walter, professor emerita at UCLA, who coined the term we chose as our title. Special thanks also to the staff at ALA Editions and Huron Street Press.

Most of all, we'd like to thank our families—especially Adreon, Joe, and Steve—for their ideas, love, and encouragement.

Introduction

FOR DECADES, LIBRARIANS HAVE LED ADULTS AND CHILDREN to stimulating discoveries, exciting imaginative adventures, and the benefits of lifelong learning. The early history of libraries tells the story of creating collections, first with clay tablets, then papyrus scrolls, and then printed books. Libraries were storehouses for religious tracts, published records, and literature. *Today a library is a portal to all human knowledge*—through printed and electronic books, music CDs, DVDs, electronic databases, and the Internet.

Books help us learn about the world, about science, and about history. They can also help us learn about ourselves. Life brings times of struggle and times of fulfillment. All families experience challenges, losses, and crises. Books can open the door to discovery for children and give them a head start in learning the art of living. Books can inspire families to explore thoughtfully, with optimism, compassion, and joy as they face the problems and challenges of life.

Ever since Beatrix Potter wrote her first book about Peter Rabbit more than 110 years ago, picture books have been a favorite choice of children. Creative and skilled authors and illustrators have filled our shelves with wonderful picture books. In recent years many of these books have dealt with *tender topics*, such as experiencing the death of a parent, telling the truth, and welcoming a new baby brother or sister. In a profound way many of these books have become the modern counterparts to Aesop's fables. They are not just stories about bunny rabbits and bears. They are books about confronting the unexpected challenges of life. In books children find characters facing struggles just as they do. They can see how the characters successfully meet difficulties. In their imagination boys and girls can learn to succeed, survive, and find peace and happiness. They can learn what to expect when faced with the unknown such as a trip to the hospital or a new baby in the household. When their story is played out in a book they enjoy, children become more comfortable with an uncertain future. Picture books can enhance children's capacity for optimism in hard times, increasing their ability to think creatively and solve problems, as well as expanding the likelihood of growing up with hope and joy and becoming their best selves.

Tender Topics examines the subjects and titles available to parents and caregivers. It helps librarians, teachers, and health-care professionals build library collections and connect parents to books. It suggests titles to empower families in approaching sensitive topics in constructive and uplifting ways. Adults can inspire lifelong enjoyment of learning and a deep capacity for problem solving in children by encouraging them to seek insight and understanding in books. We used the following criteria in selecting titles for *Tender Topics*:

> *Appeal to children*—Is the book like a banana—does it *a-peel* to children?
>
> *Subject coverage*—Does the book address the topic and explore it sensitively and intelligently?
>
> *Age level*—Is the book appropriate for preschool to elementary-school age children (with some exceptions for older children)?
>
> *Availability*—Is the book in print and readily available?
>
> *Format*—Is the book in the format of a picture book?
>
> *Perspective*—Does the book give thoughtful coverage of a topic and include a valuable perspective?
>
> *Recommendation*—Did the book receive a positive review or affirmation by a respected source, such as *School Library Journal*, *Library Journal*, *Kirkus Reviews*, *Booklist*, or the Cooperative

Children's Book Center? Or, if a title was not reviewed, does it fit our criteria for a good picture book?

Whether you are a parent, caregiver, librarian, teacher, or health-care professional, this book is designed to inspire everyone who interacts with young children as they meet life's challenges through high-quality picture books.

part I

Why Tender Topics?

Helping Children Develop the Love of Reading

THERE IS NO BETTER GIFT FOR A CHILD THAN THE LOVE OF reading. Losing yourself in a good book by letting it take you away to another place and time can be one of the great pleasures of childhood. Books that seize the imagination can help children develop a strong sense of self, as they explore characters in situations both similar to and different from their own.

Books provide a safe haven for learning about life. They can help young readers realize that others have felt the way they do or have had similar experiences. A book can be both a window and a mirror: some books let children see out to different places, cultures, and experiences, while other books allow children to see a reflection of their own experiences and feelings.[1] At their best, children's picture books awaken a young child's imagination and lead her to discover and explore the lifelong journey of learning.

In today's busy world, with its competing demands of technology, sports, and the ever-growing array of extracurricular activities, adults are rightly concerned about children's reading habits. As adults, we must inspire children to *want* to read! Research in reading motivation points to several key factors that have been proven to influence children's reading behavior, including the importance of parents and older siblings as positive role models. Other factors include being exposed to lots of books, having ready access to books, and having opportunities for choice and discussion.[2]

As an adult hoping to foster a love of reading in a child, you can begin by asking yourself the following questions:

> **Am I a positive role model when it comes to reading?** Do I actively show how much I love books by talking about them, sharing favorite books and authors, and choosing reading as a free-time activity? Do I give books as gifts on special occasions, such as birthdays and holidays, and encourage friends and relatives to do the same?

> **Do I make sure my child is exposed to lots of books by making regular visits to the library and bookstore?** Do I take advantage of storytime at the public library and ask the librarian for resource recommendations? Have I explored websites that provide access to books online? Do I read aloud to my child on a regular basis, express my enthusiasm by reading with expression, and discuss interesting parts of the book?

> **Have I made sure that my child has ready access to books?** Does my child have a bookshelf of her own? If I can't afford to buy many books, do I make regular use of the public library with my child?

> **Do I allow my child to select his own books and guide his selections at the library or bookstore?** Do I know my child's interests, so that I can ask the librarian for recommendations? If my child asks to hear the same book read aloud many times, do I honor this choice? By the same token, if my child wants to reread a favorite book, or only seems to enjoy books in a certain series for a while, do I honor those choices as well?

Do I create opportunities for my child to read, discuss, and enjoy books with others? Do we discuss books at the dinner table or other family times? Have I explored book club options suitable for my child's age?

Variations of these questions can apply to many different settings, for example, a classroom, a school media center, a child-care facility, and the public library. Children are never too old to develop a love of reading. It can be magical when a child is exposed to the right book at the right time. Keep striving toward this goal, and know that you are endowing the children in your life with a precious gift, one that will enrich their lives both now and in the years to come.

~~~~~~

Notes

1. Lee Galda, Bernice E. Cullinan, and Lawrence R. Sipe, *Literature and the Child*, 7th ed. (Belmont, CA: Wadsworth Cengage Learning, 2010), 42–44.

2. Linda Gambrell, "Creating Classroom Cultures That Foster Reading Motivation," *Reading Teacher* 50, no. 1 (1996): 15–25.

Get Your Kids Talking

READING AND TALKING ABOUT PICTURE BOOKS WITH ADULTS is one of the best ways for children to learn about life. When caring adults pose questions and present opportunities for children to talk about a story—sharing their feelings, thoughts, experiences, and insights—children can integrate the message of the book into their own thinking. For example, while reading *I Want Your Moo: A Story for Children about Self-Esteem*, you could begin a discussion by asking how the main character, Toodles the Turkey, solves her problem. This question could lead to talking about what Toodles ultimately learns and to exploring different ways the problem might be solved.

Another way to encourage conversations is to extend the story or book topic through play. For example, the story *Mrs. Biddlebox* teaches a myriad of lessons about overcoming a bad mood and invites fun and physical activity. Ask your children to play charades using phrases and action verbs from the book: *woke up on the wrong side of the bed, snatched the grass, twirled the fog, yanked the sun, stomped the mess into a dish,* and *danced*

7

while the bad mood baked into a good mood. Have your children create a plan for what they will do the next time they are in a bad mood: exercise, dance, ride their bike, sing, or bake a cake like Mrs. Biddlebox.

The relationship between an adult and a child is often like a seesaw stopped with the adult down on the ground and the child in the air. Sharing picture books together builds a stronger bond between adult and child. It is the fulcrum that allows for the kind of one-on-one interaction that can bring out a child's best creative self. A heart-to-heart intimacy breaks down the distance between adult and child as they enter the world of discovery together.

Many picture books are playful in tone. With these books, interaction is a place for spirited fun. For twenty minutes a day, or whatever time you establish, children are encouraged to express themselves, to think outside the box and have a good time. As children role-play parts of the book, invite them to act in goofy, off-the-wall ways—"Let's have fun and get silly!" Think about the time of day, though. Sharing stories at bedtime will be more low-key than sharing stories in the afternoon.

In contrast to these high-energy picture books, some tender topics books explore sensitive themes. Topics such as Death of a Parent or Loved One, New Baby, and Divorce, to name a few, may generate strong feelings when shared. Anticipating a child's reaction, planning ahead to select the best time and place to share the story, and maintaining a calm, caring, and positive demeanor are important considerations. The books in our collection provide opportunities to deal with sensitive topics in a nonthreatening, uplifting, and supportive way.

The first step in guiding children to become healthy, productive adults is to help them think for themselves. A conversation about the story can lead children toward this goal. Ideally, this exchange would be a sharing of opinions between adult and child, with no right or wrong answers: "How did you like that story?" "My favorite part was . . . What was yours?" "That character or event reminded me of . . . What did it make you think about?" Be patient at first, and before long children will be eager to share their thoughts and ideas.

Here are some tips to guide you as you encourage conversations when sharing picture books:

Take time to look at the cover and title of the book together before reading. Talk about what might happen in the story.

Read with expression and experiment with using different voices for the characters in the book.

Pick a couple of logical stopping points to engage with the story. Ask open-ended questions such as, "What do you think will happen next?" If a child needs more encouragement, comment on the events and invite a response: "Oh, I think the boy is going to help his friend now. What do you think?"

After reading, talk about the characters and events together. Invite connections to personal experiences: "What did you think about what happened? Did it remind you of anything?" If a child needs more encouragement, you could say, "This story reminds me of the first time you asked Andrew over to play. You two had such a good time together, just like the boys in the story. Do you remember what happened that day?"

Talk about any new or interesting words from the book and make a point of using the words in conversation: "The boy's mother said he was considerate. I think you were considerate this morning when you picked up your toys. Let's see how many times we can be considerate of one another this week."

The results of a 2005 study conducted by the Carroll County (Maryland) Public Library revealed the importance of encouraging conversations between caring adults and young children during picture book read-alouds. Child-care providers engaged children in conversations during storybook sharing. This verbal interaction resulted in a dramatic surge in comprehension scores. Perhaps equally important, children began to prefer this type of interactive read-aloud. They were disappointed when there was not enough time to discuss the story. This type of active engagement is the magic ingredient for creating a successful reader.

All ages will benefit from talking about books. As you explore the settings, characters, and events together, you will encourage children to become active thinkers and readers. Best of all, these conversations provide perfect opportunities to bond through the world of stories.

What Makes a Good Picture Book?

LEARNING IS MEANT TO BE A LIFELONG ENDEAVOR. LEARNING the art of living will give young children a strong foundation. The way they grapple with unexpected challenges and important life experiences—with tender topics—will help determine their ability to lead full and enriching lives. Picture books offer opportunities for families to discuss challenges and to build upon the enjoyment of learning.

Picture books are a relatively new addition to the world of publishing. In the 1870s and 1880s, the talented illustrator Randolph Caldecott created a book format in which the words and pictures were equally important and necessary for telling the story. Early best sellers, such as Beatrix Potter's *The Tale of Peter Rabbit* (1902), paved the way for the publishing world to embrace the picture book. The industry has gone through waves of expansion, with new technology allowing any art medium to be reproduced as a picture book. The result is that we now have a wealth of high-quality picture books, representing many genres and topics, to enrich the lives of children—and the adults who care for them.

A good picture book is much more than words with illustrations. Excellence in a picture book is related to the artfulness of the book as a whole. The following criteria for evaluating picture books are adapted from *Literature and the Child* by Lee Galda, Bernice Cullinan, and Lawrence Sipe.[1]

All Picture Books

- Language is rich, with interesting words used in interesting ways.
- Illustrations are artistically excellent.
- Size, shape, and overall design of the book are appropriate to the subject or story.

Fiction

- Text and illustrations establish the mood, setting, characters, and theme of the story.
- Illustrations expand on the story appropriately and do not merely duplicate what is described in the text.
- Layout and design are visually appealing.

Nonfiction

- Text and illustrations are:
  accurate
  organized in an appropriate manner
  attractive
- Text and illustrations show verve and style.

In his introduction to *Show Me a Story! Why Picture Books Matter*, renowned illustrator David Wiesner reminds us that the first art most children see is in picture books.[2] This is a big responsibility, one that the most talented illustrators do not take lightly. Illustrators rely on certain principles of design to enhance meaning in an artfully composed picture book. These principles help us evaluate how the illustrations support and extend the text. Galda, Cullinan, and Sipe have summarized the following principles of design detailed in *Picture This: How Pictures Work* by Molly Bang.[3]

- Smooth, flat, horizontal shapes present a sense of stability and calm.
- Vertical shapes are more exciting and active, implying energy and reaching.
- Diagonal shapes are dynamic, implying motion or tension.
- The upper half of a picture connotes freedom, happiness, triumph, and spirituality.
- The bottom half connotes strength, heaviness, sadness, and constraint.
- An object in the upper half carries greater pictorial weight and emphasis.
- The center of the page is the point of greatest attraction.
- White or light backgrounds feel safer than dark ones.
- Pointed shapes frighten; rounded shapes and curves comfort and feel safe.
- The larger an object, the stronger it feels, whereas the smaller an object, the weaker or more insignificant it seems.
- Contrast enables us to see more clearly.

For this book, we strove to select a sampling of the best in children's picture books pertaining to tender topics. Our titles include some classics but focus more on recent works. All were readily available in print at the time of our writing. The topics have been arranged in order of likely interest to children, and within each topic, books are listed in order of preference. Leaders in the field of children's literature, such as the American Library Association (ALA), the Association for Library Service to Children (ALSC), the Cooperative Children's Book Center (CCBC), *School Library Journal*, and others, have guided our choices. The books we have selected offer the opportunity to explore sensitive issues in an uplifting manner, within the comforting realm of storybook sharing.

Notes

1. Lee Galda, Bernice E. Cullinan, and Lawrence R. Sipe, *Literature and the Child*, 7th ed. (Belmont, CA: Wadsworth Cengage Learning, 2010), 127.

2. David Weisner, introduction to *Show Me a Story! Why Picture Books Matter*, by Leonard S. Marcus (Somerville, MA: Candlewick, 2012).

3. Galda et al., *Literature and the Child*, 71.

part II

Selections on Tender Topics

4

Friendship

FRIENDSHIPS CAN BE A GREAT SOURCE OF COMFORT AND SUP-
port for young and old alike. The capacity to make and
keep friends is an important part of a child's social and
emotional development. Shared interests provide a good
starting point for a lasting friendship, so helping children explore a variety of pastimes is helpful. Encourag-
ing curiosity about art, music, sports, the outdoors, and so forth, can give
children many opportunities to bond with others who share their interests. Having the opportunity to play with others is also helpful for forming
friendships in the preschool years. The books in this chapter explore how
to get along with others, and the qualities needed to make friends and
keep them.

Yes We Can!

By Sam McBratney. Illustrated by Charles Fuge. HarperCollins, 2007.
Good friends Roo, Mouse, and Duck are having fun making a mountain of
leaves together. That is, until they begin to tease one another about something one of them can't do. Soon all three are in a bad mood. Enter Roo's

mother, who gently chides them for laughing at one other. She suggests they show each other what they *can* do. Each takes a turn, and frowns quickly turn to smiles. When Roo's mom asks if the playmates can be friends again, the title states their unanimous reply. McBratney's skill at depicting childhood friendships is evident in this engaging tale.

I'm Sorry

By Sam McBratney. Illustrated by Jennifer Eachus. HarperCollins, 2000.
Two preschoolers have fun playing school and teaching their toys to read, splashing in rain puddles, and making each other laugh. Then one day they shout at each other. Now the best friends refuse to speak, pretending they can't see each other. The magic words *I'm sorry* make everything better once again. The softly hued watercolor illustrations add to the calming effect for little ones.

Bears on Chairs

By Shirley Parenteau. Illustrated by David Walker. Candlewick, 2009.
Little bears learn to share in this charming picture book for little ones. Four bears and four chairs work perfectly until Big Brown Bear comes along. Now what will the friends do? Never fear, they solve the problem by pushing all the chairs together. Now, there's room for all five bears! This little story makes a sweet introduction to sharing for young children.

Being Friends

By Karen Beaumont. Illustrated by Joy Allen. Dial, 2002.
Two very different little girls celebrate their friendship in this delightful rhyming story. "You are you and I am me. You're a princess sipping tea. I'm a swinging chimpanzee." Allen's lively illustrations complement the joyous text.

You Will Be My Friend!

By Peter Brown. Illustrated by the author. Little, Brown, 2011.
The exuberant Lucy sets out to make a new friend. The little bear meets many forest critters, and each seems like a perfect choice to her. She tries

hard to win the animals over, but something always goes wrong. Poor Lucy just doesn't fit in with anyone. Puzzled and annoyed, she starts demanding that everyone be her friend. As all the animals run away from her, she cries in frustration. Only then does a new creature find her and ask to be her friend. The comical illustrations and tongue-in-cheek treatment of how to make a friend form a winning combination.

I'm the Best
By Lucy Cousins. Illustrated by the author. Candlewick, 2010.
A boastful, but lovable, dog brags to all of his friends that he is the best at everything. All of his friends become sad until they realize that they can do many things better than Dog. Dog then becomes contrite for having been mean to his friends. His friends rush to console him by telling him he is a good friend and is the best at having beautiful, fluffy ears. Dog again proclaims he is the best. The brightly colored illustrations leap off the page in this comic story. Children will appreciate both the humor and the message.

Zen Ties
By Jon J Muth. Illustrated by the author. Scholastic Press, 2008.
Friendship and compassion for others are celebrated in this beautiful story. Stillwater, the giant panda, introduces his friends Addy, Michael, and Karl to his nephew, Koo. He then encourages all to visit a grumpy, elderly lady, who happens to be a retired teacher in need of companionship. The children have always been afraid of Miss Whitaker, and at first she lives up to her reputation. Through Stillwater's gentle guidance, the children and Miss Whitaker come to appreciate and help one another. A rich story with many layers of meaning, this book has something to offer all age groups.

A Sick Day for Amos McGee
By Philip C. Stead. Illustrated by Erin E. Stead. Roaring Brook, 2010.
Amos McGee, the zookeeper, never misses a day of work. He always has time for his animal friends, sitting quietly with them, reading to them, and providing handkerchiefs for runny noses. When he becomes sick with a

bad cold, his friends miss him terribly. Together, they set off across town to visit him. A sweet and humorous tale of friendship and kindness, this story will impress children with its message, memorable characters, and expressive illustrations.

How to Be a Friend:
A Guide to Making Friends and Keeping Them

By Laurie Krasny Brown. Illustrated by Marc Brown. Little, Brown, 1998.
Cartoonlike characters in the form of dinosaur children present a guide for making and keeping friends. The combination of informational text and creatures conversing using speech bubbles creates a novel take on a non-fiction subject. Among the topics are "Ways to Be a Friend," "Feeling Shy," "Talking Out an Argument," and "Being Friendly."

A Very Big Bunny

By Marisabina Russo. Illustrated by the author. Schwartz and Wade, 2010.
Amelia is the biggest bunny in her class. This presents many challenges on the playground, as her feet are too big for hopscotch and the seesaw is impossible. Her loving parents try to help by telling her that she stands out in a crowd and will always be the star of the show, but Amelia just wants to be a not-so-big bunny. Then Susannah, a very small bunny, joins her class. Eventually, the two become friends as they learn to appreciate each other's unique qualities. The resolution provides an uplifting conclusion to this honest portrayal of how it feels to be different.

Same, Same, but Different

By Jenny Sue Kostecki-Shaw. Illustrated by the author. Henry Holt, 2011.
Elliot, from America, and Kailash, from India, are pen pals. Exchanging letters and pictures, they learn about each other and their worlds. The vibrant illustrations and enthusiastic descriptions show the reader that their lives are different, but the same. This engaging story has many applications beyond the theme of friendship.

Poindexter Makes a Friend

By Mike Twohy. Illustrated by the author. Simon and Schuster, 2011.
Poindexter, a shy little pig, hides under the carpet when relatives come to visit. When kids in his neighborhood ask him to play, he makes up an excuse not to join them. Poindexter enjoys reading to his stuffed animals.

His favorite place to go is the public library, where he can sit by himself and read. When Mrs. Polen, the librarian, gives him a job at the front desk, Poindexter finds himself helping a shy turtle read a book called *How to Make a Friend*. As you can imagine, the two learn together and become friends.

Chester's Way
By Kevin Henkes. Illustrated by the author. Greenwillow, 1988.
Chester has a mind of his own. He likes to play croquet and eat peanut butter and make his bed. Chester and Wilson are the best of friends, as alike as two peas in a pod. They do everything exactly the same way until Lilly moves into the neighborhood. Lily has a mind of her own, too, and she is completely different from Chester and Wilson, or so they think. The three find out they have a lot in common, despite their differences. The endearing mouse characters will have everyone smiling in this celebration of childhood and friendship.

City Dog, Country Frog
By Mo Willems. Illustrated by Jon J Muth. Hyperion, 2010.
City Dog is delighted to find himself in the country, free to run without a leash. H e soon finds a new friend, Country Frog. Each season finds them playing together and teaching one another a new game. One fall day, Dog finds his friend, only to discover that Frog is too tired to explore and play. The two friends sit and play remembering games. Winter comes and Dog misses his friend. Spring arrives, and he makes a new friend, Country Chipmunk. A touching, understated picture of friendship and loss, this is an excellent choice for sharing with children who have lost a friend through illness or moving.

I Love My New Toy!
By Mo Willems. Illustrated by the author. Hyperion, 2008.
Gerald and Piggie are best friends—that is, until Gerald breaks Piggie's new toy. The range of emotions Willems portrays on the characters' faces is priceless, as they go through being mad, sad, ashamed, apologetic, and, finally, embarrassed. The embarrassment is on Piggie's part when Squirrel announces that the toy is a break-and-snap toy. The delightful ending has the two friends realizing that playing together is much more fun than having a new toy.

Squish Rabbit

By Katherine Battersby. Illustrated by the author. Viking, 2011.
Squish is a little rabbit in a big world. Lonely for companionship, he makes a stuffed rabbit for a pretend friend. This helps some, but not enough. Just as he is throwing a tantrum, a little squirrel peeks out of a tree. Now Squish has a friend his size. Preschoolers will delight in this simple yet charming picture book, with its strong message of friendship.

How Do Dinosaurs Play with Their Friends?

By Jane Yolen. Illustrated by Mark Teague. Blue Sky, 2006.
In Yolen and Teague's popular How Do Dinosaurs series for young children, lovable dinosaur characters promote good behavior by showing the naughty counterpoint. This book reveals the proper way to play with friends by asking questions that will delight children by their playfulness. "Does he hide all his dump trucks, refusing to share? Does he throw his friends' coloring books in the air?" The last pages always reveal how to be a good little dinosaur.

The Sandwich Swap

By Her Majesty Queen Rania Al Abdullah with Kelly DiPucchio. Illustrated by Tricia Tusa. Disney-Hyperion, 2010.
Lily and Salma do a lot of things together because they are best friends. Every day at school they eat lunch together; Lily always eats a peanut butter and jelly sandwich, and Salma always eats a hummus and pita sandwich. Silently, each thinks the other's sandwich is strange and gross. When their thoughts are spoken, the girls argue. Classmates overhear, and soon everyone is name-calling. The story ends happily when the students have an international picnic and come to appreciate their differences. Inspired by the Queen of Jordan's own childhood, this child-friendly story teaches cross-cultural tolerance and acceptance.

Sam's New Friend

By Thierry Robberecht. Illustrated by Philippe Goossens. Clarion, 2007.
Sam is a puppy who thinks that boys are tough and girls are not. Then Sam's mom invites the new girl home after school. Ellie is her friend's daughter, and the little kitten is quiet and sad. Sam tries to comfort her and soon learns why Ellie is sad—her parents may be getting a divorce.

Sam plays with his new friend at school the next day and doesn't mind when the other boys stare. Ellie doesn't know what will happen with her parents, but Sam knows she will be all right because Ellie is tough and brave, just like him.

Marshall Armstrong Is New to Our School

By David Mackintosh. Illustrated by the author. Abrams, 2011.
Marshall Armstrong is different from everyone in his new school. The narrator, who sits next to him in class, describes Marshall as having freckles that look like birdseed and ears like seashells. He eats "space food" wrapped in silver wrappers, is not allowed to play sports or watch television, and has to stay in the shade outside. Unfazed by what others think of him, Marshall invites everyone to his birthday party. The narrator then describes the most amazing birthday party ever at the Armstrong home. Mackintosh's unique take on being the new kid and making friends is highly engaging.

The Berenstain Bears and the Trouble with Friends

Written and illustrated by Stan and Jan Berenstain. Random House, 1986.
Sister Bear is excited to see a little girl cub move in next door. When Sister goes to Lizzy's house to play school, they argue over which of them will be the teacher. They part ways in a huff, with Sister shouting that she never wants to see her new friend again. Wise Mama Bear helps Sister see that playing by herself so she can have everything her own way can be pretty lonesome. The happy resolution has the new friends agreeing to take turns being teacher. This time-tested series is still an engaging choice for young children.

5

Resiliency

PART OF NURTURING CHILDREN'S GROWTH IS INSPIRING THEM to be their best selves. For example, children build confidence as they learn from their mistakes. They discover that becoming successful in life, as a student or friend or parent or businessperson, involves trial and error. They develop skills and abilities—such as perseverance, optimism, and determination—that will help them be their best selves as they face each new challenge or opportunity.

Pete the Cat: I Love My White Shoes

By Eric Litwin (aka Mr. Eric). Illustrated by James Dean. HarperCollins, 2010.

What do you do when you walk into a pile of strawberries and stain your brand-new white shoes? Do you cry? "Goodness, no!" says Pete the Cat. He keeps walking and singing his song because now he loves his red shoes. Do you cry when you walk into a pile of blueberries or a large mud puddle? Pete the Cat is supremely flexible and makes the most of each potential disaster. The richly colored artwork is a perfect match for this interactive, fun-filled book.

Perfect Square

By Michael Hall. Illustrated by the author. Greenwillow, 2011.

How do you handle yourself when you have a bad day? How do you grapple with being cut into pieces, poked full of holes, torn into scraps, or shredded into strips? The perfect square doesn't stay unhappy for long; it makes itself into a fountain that babbles and giggles or into a garden or a park! Follow the red square as it faces a new challenge each day and renews itself by changing color, shape, and design. Hall has created a brilliant picture book that will inspire children—and adults—to turn problems into opportunities.

Perfect Piggies! A Book! A Song! A Celebration! (a board book)

By Sandra Boynton. Illustrated by the author. Workman, 2010.

This board book for infants and toddlers stands out as a source for helping children create a healthy self-image. Boynton, a prolific children's author, songwriter, and cartoonist, is a genius at tapping into the joy of life. Cows may be more intelligent. Ducks may be more fashionable. Pigs, however, are perfect! Their ears are "floppy and fine." Their noses are "wonderfully round." Every page will delight children with quirky fun and upbeat illustrations. A free downloadable song accompanies this burst of celebration.

Olivia

By Ian Falconer. Illustrated by the author. Atheneum, 2000.

Precocious and dauntless, Olivia the pig sails through her day dragging her mother, father, and baby brother with her. She brushes her teeth, tries on many gorgeous outfits, basks in the sun at the beach, and makes amazing sand castles. After avoiding her nap, Olivia visits the museum, where she ponders the beauty of her

favorite painting and puzzles over another one. She dashes home to try *her* hand at painting—on the wall of her bedroom. After time-out, it's time to bathe and eat dinner. Olivia becomes a fearless negotiator, convincing her mother to read aloud three storybooks before bedtime. Whew!

Tacky the Penguin

By Helen Lester. Illustrated by Lynn Munsinger. Houghton Mifflin, 1988.
Tacky is not like his penguin pals, Goodly, Lovely, Angel, Neatly, and Perfect. Tacky greets others boisterously, marches in a zigzag loop, jumps cannonball style splashing everyone in the pool, and sings loudly, proudly—and off-key. He's considered an odd bird until one day his quirkiness distracts a group of penguin hunters, thus saving his friends. The witty and funny text will invite children to act out each scene of the story. Munsinger's expressive and adorable illustrations illuminate Lester's charming Tacky the Penguin. The odd bird in all of us will flutter its wings with delight.

Walter, the Farting Dog

By William Kotzwinkle and Glenn Murray. Illustrated by Audrey Colman. Frog, 2001.

This hilarious story, cowritten by Kotzwinkle of *E.T., the Extra-Terrestrial* fame, should strengthen anyone's sense of self, though not all adults will approve. Walter, an apologetic-looking dog adopted at the pound, has a flatulence problem. "No matter what that dog eats, he turns it into farts," roars Father. Walter must go back to the pound. However, on Walter's last night his farting creates a gas cloud that stops a pair of burglars in their tracks. The quirky illustrations fit perfectly with the witty text. A family hero now, Walter can, at last, fart proudly!

Ernest, the Moose Who Doesn't Fit

By Catherine Rayner. Illustrated by the author. Farrar Straus Giroux, 2010.
This simple and engaging vignette demonstrates the positive results of being determined. Ernest the Moose is too big to fit on the page of the book. With assistance from his little chipmunk friend, Ernest resolves to take on the challenge. The two persistent problem-solvers think out-

side the box—or outside the book, if you will—and fix Ernest's dilemma. Rayner has created a fun and clever story with a big ending!

The Little Engine That Could

Adapted by Watty Piper. Illustrated by Loren Long. Philomel, 2005.
This classic tale will reinforce the concepts of perseverance, hard work, and goodwill. Little Blue Engine, who has never been over the mountain, takes a risk to help the children on the other side. She puffs and chugs, "I think I can—I think I can." As she reaches the top of the mountain, the clown cries with joy. The cheerful illustrations will charm children as they follow Little Blue Engine to eventual triumph!

I Want Your Moo: A Story for Children about Self-Esteem

By Marcella Bakur Weiner and Jill Neimark. Illustrated by JoAnn Adinolfi. Magination, 2010.
This lighthearted self-help picture book will resonate with children who may not like part of themselves. The cheerful illustrations and sing-song rhythm of the text match the book's message to appreciate and respect our own strengths and potential. Toodles the Turkey doesn't value her gobble-gobble and tries to acquire the sounds of other animals, including the pig's oink, the duck's quack, the horse's neigh, and the cow's moo. One day Toodles yells her gobble-gobble sound and successfully protects the barnyard chicks from a circling hawk. She realizes and now treasures that this is the way she was "always meant to be."

All by Myself!

By Aliki. Illustrated by the author. HarperCollins, 2000.
A little boy exudes excitement from the moment he wakes up until it's time to say good night. He is learning to be independent and can do many things already. He brushes his teeth, takes off his pajamas, buttons and zips his blue jeans, and puts on socks and shoes. It's time for a flip, then on to breakfast. At preschool the boy builds, sings, writes, and paints. Afterward, he plays with friends, goes to the library, helps with dinner, takes a bath, reads stories, and finally stops! The adorable watercolors and playful, rhyming text will motivate children to be independent too.

Are You a Cow? (a board book)

By Sandra Boynton. Illustrated by the author. Little Simon, 2012.
Hey! What are you—a duck, a lamb, a dog, or a frog? Are you a cow, a hippo, or a pig? No, you are none of these, because you are not big. "Wait! You must be you! Now isn't that great!" A chicken narrates this delightful rhyming board book for infants and toddlers by the remarkable Sandra Boynton.

The Little Chapel That Stood

By A. B. Curtiss. Illustrated by Mirto Golino. Oldcastle, 2003.
What better model of resiliency than America's spirit after September 11? Curtiss ties the history of St. Paul's Church, where George Washington and his family worshipped, to its improbable escape from the falling Twin Towers—*not a brick out of place*. This true story offers an easy way for adults to discuss with young children the devastation of September 11 and the courage and resilience of a country.

If You're Happy and You Know It . . . / Si te sientes bien contento . . . (a board book in Spanish and English)

By Annie Kubler. Illustrated by the author. Child's Play International, 2009.
Part of an award-winning series, this board book will delight babies and adults alike. Using the well-known children's song, "If You're Happy and You Know It," Kubler has created a charming interactive experience. Each page is filled with joy and features warm illustrations and fun action cues: clap your hands, kick your legs, shake and rattle, and roll about. Learning opportunities for babies abound! They can listen to playful language, develop their motor skills, and strengthen their bond with their parents, all of which help them create a better sense of self.

If You're Happy and You Know It, Jungle Edition

By James Warhola. Illustrated by the author. Orchard, 2007.
In this version of the classic song, Warhola takes children into a jungle playground fantasy. Children learn to stomp their feet with the elephants, give a roar with the lions, scratch their fur with the monkeys, and laugh out loud with the hyenas. The watercolors drip with action and good cheer. Along with the pragmatic aspect of developing motor skills, the illustrations perfect the experience of sheer fun. Children and adults will jump for joy.

The Tortoise and the Hare: An Aesop Fable

Adapted and illustrated by Janet Stevens. Holiday House, 1984.
Stevens has created a modern classic picture book by retelling a timeless tale. Her warm and expressive artwork matches her storytelling ability. The well-known race springs to life as we follow the tortoise and the hare to the finish line. Overconfident Hare pauses to sip lemonade, munch on snacks, and gloat about how easily he'll beat Tortoise. Striving to do his steady best, Tortoise marches forward a step at a time. Hare is blinded by the glamour he has created around his inability to fail. After boldly taking a nap, Hare wakes up to find it's too late—Tortoise has, not surprisingly, won the race.

Big Plans

By Bob Shea. Illustrated by Lane Smith. Hyperion, 2008.
Given a time-out in class, a little boy uses his imagination to ponder, concoct, and explore his big plans. Thus begins this marvelous journey into the realm of "anything is possible"—running a business, winning the football game, becoming town mayor and even president. Inspired by the classroom's books and resources, the little boy befriends a mynah bird as his sidekick, creates a stinky lucky hat out of a skunk, and directs Pennsylvania to build rocket ships and Idaho to make space suits "using the latest potato technology." Children will be inspired to create their own big plans!

Harold and the Purple Crayon, 50th Anniversary Edition

By Crockett Johnson. Illustrated by the author. HarperCollins, 2005.
Harold and his crayon have inspired children to use their imaginations since the book's release in 1955. Join Harold on his purple adventures as he draws himself a moon, a path, a forest, an ocean, and a hot air balloon. Johnson's streamlined design encourages young children to explore their creativity and ideas about the world.

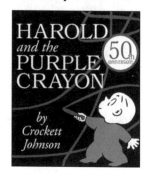

Not a Box

By Antoinette Portis. Illustrated by the author. HarperCollins, 2006.
A simple object like a box can unleash a child's imagination. Portis's simple line drawings and charming text tell the story of a bunny creating his own adventures using a cardboard box. An unenlightened questioner asks why

our imaginative hero is sitting in a box or wearing a box or standing in a box. The bunny replies, "It's not a box," as the box turns into a race car or a boat or a robot or a basket on top of an elephant. Inside his box, the bunny can let his imagination run wild, gaining insight into the world around him.

The Princess and the Moon

By Daisaku Ikeda. Illustrated by Brian Wildsmith. English version by Geraldine McCaughrean. Knopf, 1992.

Brian Wildsmith, illustrator and a Kate Greenaway medalist, and Daisaku Ikeda, educator and Buddhist philosopher, teamed up to create this amazing book about children learning about and practicing helpfulness, cheerfulness, and patience. A Great Rabbit leaps from a moonbeam to earth and takes Sophie on a journey to see the moon's country where little boys and girls are their perfect selves. Sophie is relieved that she is not going to be punished for being bad-tempered or naughty in school, but instead is encouraged to discover how easy it is to smile and be kind to others.

Harris Finds His Feet

By Catherine Rayner. Illustrated by the author. Good Books, 2008.

Harris the hare sighs as he wonders out loud why his feet are so enormous. His grandfather smiles and takes Harris on an adventure to learn the many reasons why: to hop high in the sky, to climb to the tallest mountains, to dig a cool resting spot, and to run very fast. Harris eventually learns to run on his own and discover the world around him. Rayner's lively illustrations make Harris's journey all the more delightful.

Augustus and His Smile

By Catherine Rayner. Illustrated by the author. Good Books, 2006.

When you lose your smile, do you search high and low? Do you look far and wide, only to discover that your smile is within you all the time? Augustus, a beautiful, strong tiger, takes the reader through an intriguing journey, coming across a beetle in the bushes, birds in the trees, snow clouds atop the mountains, and tiny, shiny fish in the ocean. Then as he enjoys a rainfall and looks into a puddle of water, he notices his smile is right under his nose. Rayner's smile shines through each page!

I Hate English!

By Ellen Levine. Illustrated by Steve Björkman. Scholastic, 1989.

This ALA Children's Notable Book confronts how difficult it can be to change, in this case from thinking and speaking in Chinese to doing so in English. Mei Mei refuses to speak English after her family moves from Hong Kong to Chinatown in New York City. One day the new teacher at the learning center insists on going out for a walk with Mei Mei. The teacher blathers on about her favorite book and how she loves potatoes. Mei Mei can't stand it anymore and shouts, "I want to talk!" and does so in English for the next twenty-one minutes!

The Quiet Book

By Deborah Underwood. Illustrated by Renata Liwska. Houghton Mifflin, 2010.

Quiet reflection time can be an essential part of life—such as the times when you make a wish, are the first one to wake up, color in the lines, and enjoy the first snowfall of the season. Other types of quiets are important too—sleeping sister, don't scare the robin, and before the concert quiets. Have you thought of other quiet times? Thinking of a good reason for drawing on the wall or having a surprise visit from Aunt Tillie or trying not to hiccup? Adults and children will enjoy the gently rendered artwork depicting charming animal characters in this reflective and funny book.

Try and Stick with It

By Cheri J. Meiners. Illustrated by Meredith Johnson. Free Spirit, 2004.

Playing baseball, learning a musical instrument, riding a bicycle, and flying a kite are some of the things that children want to try. How can adults help children discover and practice courage, patience, and cheerfulness as they try new things? Meiners fosters several practical skills to cultivate perseverance, such as finish what you start, imagine yourself doing it, do it a step at a time, take a break, and try it with a new approach. The handsome illustrations happily complement the stick-to-it-isms. The activity ideas in the back of the book will encourage your child to try and stick with it.

Life Lessons

GENEROSITY, INTEGRITY, AND RESOURCEFULNESS ARE A FEW of the virtues that enable children to grow into discerning, purposeful, and caring adults. Fables and folk tales have traditionally offered lessons that build character. A classic life lesson, "Don't believe everything you hear," can be found in the compelling story "The Rooster and the Fox" in Aesop's fables. *The Last Puppy* by Frank Asch is an excellent example of how *not* to make oneself miserable. Stories give children the opportunity to explore subtle but significant lessons. While listening to a story, children use their imaginations to rehearse how they might handle a similar situation.

Boxes for Katje
By Candace Fleming. Illustrated by Stacey Dressen-McQueen. Farrar Straus Giroux, 2003.
The generous spirit of the residents of Mayfield, Indiana, inspired Fleming to tell her mother's childhood story. Rosie became pen pals with Katje of

Olst, Holland, after World War II. Rosie sent soap, socks, and chocolate along with a letter: "I hope these gifts brighten your day." This simple act started a chain of events that led to the town of Mayfield pitching in to help the town of Olst with much-needed supplies of coats, hats, shoes, sweaters, and cans of food to get through the winter. After surviving the winter, Katje sent a box of tulip bulbs from Olst to "brighten Mayfield's days."

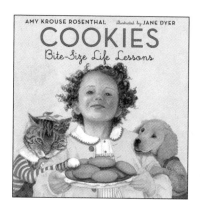

Cookies: Bite-Size Life Lessons

By Amy Krouse Rosenthal. Illustrated by Jane Dyer. HarperCollins, 2006.

Did you know that baking cookies is like learning the art of living? They both require dynamic qualities: cooperation in preparing the dough, patience as the cookies bake, pride in how they turn out, generosity in sharing them with others, and contentment in eating them. Some of the two-page spreads complement each other—for example, honesty about who took the cookie (it wasn't really the butterfly) and the courage to speak up. Another example—one of our favorites—pairs pessimism about having only half a cookie left with optimism about still having half a cookie left. Dyer's soft illustrations help make this a standard for every home and library.

A Child's Garden of Verses

By Robert Louis Stevenson. Illustrated by Brian Wildsmith. Star Bright, 2008.

Award-winning Wildsmith captures the joy, adventure, and beauty of Stevenson's poems in this colorfully illustrated collection for children. Discover what it's like to whiz along looking out "From a Railway Carriage." Observe how a trout disturbs the surface of the water, creating concentric circles that spread out until they fade away in "Looking-Glass River." Enjoy trees, sheep, flying fairies, and more in "Picture Books in Winter." Stevenson's poetry will expand your horizons, enrich your child, and delight you both. "Happy Thought: The world is full of a number of things, / I'm sure we should all be as happy as kings."

Something from Nothing

By Phoebe Gilman. Illustrated by the author. Scholastic, 1992.

The warm illustrations and spirit-lifting text make this adaptation of a traditional Jewish folktale about resourcefulness a delight with each turn of the page. Grandpa sews Joseph a beautiful blue blanket to keep him warm and "chase away bad dreams." The blanket becomes old and must be thrown out, but Grandpa fixes it by sewing it into a jacket! The jacket becomes too small, but Grandpa fixes it again by creating a vest, then a tie, a handkerchief, and finally a button. When the button is lost, Joseph fixes it by writing this beautiful story. Children will also enjoy the mouse family's story within a story.

The Monster That Grew Small: An Egyptian Folktale

Adapted by Joan Grant. Illustrated by Jill Karla Schwarz. Lothrop, Lee and Shepard, 1987.

One of life's great lessons is learning that fears seem to shrink once they are faced. Miobi, a boy in ancient Egypt known as the "Frightened One," untangles a rabbit caught by a creeper bush. The magical rabbit returns Miobi's kindness by giving sage advice each time Miobi is afraid. Miobi learns to scare the crocodiles and outwit the serpents. He comes upon a village that is enslaved to anxiety about a monster on the mountain. Miobi climbs the mountain to discover that the monster, What-Might-Happen, grows smaller with each step and becomes quite manageable. The illustrations are beautiful and lighthearted.

The Little Red Hen

Adapted and illustrated by Paul Galdone. Clarion, 2006.

Sharing in the work means sharing the reward. The cat, the dog, and the mouse are downright lazy. Little Red Hen's friends refuse to help her plant, tend, and cut the wheat and grind it into flour. Still she doesn't give up on them and asks for their help to bake bread. "Not I!" is the unanimous response once again. When the bread is ready, Hen doesn't share it. In the end, she reaps the reward for her effort. She also teaches her friends a lesson—share in the work. Galdone's lively illustrations make this classic a favorite with children.

The McElderry Book of Aesop's Fables

Adapted by Michael Morpurgo. Illustrated by Emma Chichester Clark. Margaret K. McElderry, 2005.

The warm, cartoonlike illustrations perfectly match the clear and pleasing modern text in this rendition of twenty-one fables in the tradition of Aesop. The brilliant stories reveal thought-provoking lessons, such as the disastrous result when the stubborn oak tree will not bend in the storm and the farmer's disappointment when he realizes his greedy mistake of killing the goose that laid the golden eggs. When the sun and the wind compete to persuade a traveler to remove his cloak, the gentle, steady source of sunlight wins over the intermittent force of wind gusts. These tales will get kids laughing and thinking—a winning combination.

The Empty Pot

By Demi. Illustrated by the author. Henry Holt, 1990.

The Emperor seeks a successor and holds a flower-growing contest to make his selection. All children shall show their best effort using a special seed given by the Emperor. Ping carefully nurtures his seed in a pot, but it does not grow. In the spring everyone shows off their flowers except Ping. He presents an empty pot, disclosing it was the best he could do. The Emperor reveals that his special seeds were cooked and impossible to sprout. Ping is "the one person worthy of being Emperor." Demi's warm and detailed artwork reflects the essence of honesty in this lovely Chinese proverb.

The Fantastic Flying Books of Mr. Morris Lessmore

By William Joyce. Illustrated by William Joyce and Joe Bluhm. Atheneum, 2012.

Do you hear the whisper from books inviting you to adventure? Do you get lost in a book and don't emerge for days? Do you like to share books with others? William Joyce takes the reader on a journey to discover that "everyone's story matters." This innovative book about books, libraries, reading, and writing stimulates the imagination as it celebrates the importance of story. The development of the character Morris Lessmore began as an accolade to Bill Morris, a pioneer of library promotions. The story inspired the short film by the same name that won a 2012 Academy Award.

The Invisible String

By Patrice Karst. Illustrated by Geoff Stevenson. DeVorss, 2000.
Karst's delightful story centers on how love creates strong connections and is ever-expanding. Liza and Jeremy are suddenly awakened by a thunderstorm. Their mother seizes the opportunity to teach them about the power of love. Love, she says, travels along an invisible string and can be felt in the heart. The children ask if the string can reach them if they are climbing a mountain or exploring a jungle. Does it go away when their mother is "mad" at them? Can it reach their Uncle Brian in heaven? She explains that love is stronger than anger and can reach "anywhere and everywhere."

This Is the Sunflower

By Lola M. Schaefer. Illustrated by Donald Crews. Greenwillow, 2000.
Prolific author Lola Schaefer—with over 250 published books—teams with award-winning artist Donald Crews to create this brilliant narrative nonfiction title about the life cycle of a sunflower. The exuberant rhyming text dances playfully within the richly colored artwork. A clever technique traces the cycle of life to discover the origin of the sunflowers—"a few seeds scattered around, spilled by the birds, full of song"—and creates an intriguing adventure. The broader lesson that we are each part of life's cycle inspires children to appreciate, indeed relish, each stage of growth.

The Hour Glass: Sixty Fables for This Moment in Time

By Carl Japikse. Illustrated by Mark Peyton. Ariel, 1984.
The Hour Glass charmed the socks off us. Mark Peyton's illustrations distinctively complement the collection of stories. Japikse's fables entertain and encourage older children to develop an insatiable sense of discovery and to tap their innate impulse to learn. Through the story of two brothers, we learn about using the mind to think through a problem and the heart to express generosity. A stagnant lake transforms itself by reuniting with its source, a sparkling river, and then shares its gifts with the barren valley

below. Many of the best character-building attributes are presented in this treasure trove of human qualities: patience, confidence, self-reliance, helpfulness, humility, harmony, and joy.

King Midas: The Golden Touch

By Demi. Illustrated by the author. Margaret K. McElderry, 2002.

Award-winning children's book author and artist Demi tells the story of self-centered King Midas and his transformation into a generous and wise person. King Midas does foolish things. He is punished by Apollo, yet he continues to make poor choices. He asks Dionysus to give him the ability to turn everything he touches into gold, with disastrous results. The spell is lifted when King Midas bathes in the river of gold, and he begins to understand the true meaning of abundance. Children will be enchanted with the story and will enjoy the richly detailed and brightly colored illustrations.

The Rainbow Goblins

By Ul de Rico. Illustrated by the author. Thames and Hudson, new edition, 1994.

The stunning artwork captures the expansive quality of abundance. Children will enjoy the lush color and rich detail in the hidden Valley of the Rainbow: horses, elephants, lions, tigers, giraffes, birds, trees, grasses, rivers, lakes, and flowers. The moon spreads the word after spotting seven greedy goblins coming to the valley to steal the Rainbow. The goblins sleep in a cave and dream of drinking the "succulent" colors of the Rainbow. In the morning the flowers ensnarl and destroy the greedy goblins as they try to lasso the Rainbow. The Valley of the Rainbow becomes stronger and more magnificent.

Plant a Kiss

By Amy Krouse Rosenthal. Illustrated by Peter H. Reynolds. HarperCollins, 2012.

What better way to spread love than by planting kisses! Little Miss plants a kiss in the ground. She waters it, nurtures it, and watches it grow into the beautiful, sparkling energy of love. Little Miss ignores her friends' advice that the kiss will "go bare" if she shares it. She picks the magical kiss and puts it into a bowl. Returning after a worldwide journey of sharing the energy of love, she discovers that her kiss continues to grow and that love is endless. The artwork is simple yet uplifting.

America Is—

By Louise Borden. Illustrated by Stacey Schuett. Margaret K. McElderry, 2002.

Prolific children's author Louise Borden defines America as "the nation whose name means freedom to people all over the world." Borden developed the idea for the book while visiting England, where a young student asked, "What's it like to live in America?" Throughout this book, Borden's answer salutes this great country. Beautiful countrysides and cityscapes, rivers and bayous, and mountains and deserts are part of America. It is a place to be productive and to have fun. It is a place to join other Americans and to connect with others around the world in the name of freedom. Schuett's sweeping illustrations will lift children into the spirit of America.

Johnny Appleseed

By Jodie Shepherd. Illustrated by Masumi Furukawa. Scholastic, 2010.

Johnny Appleseed—born John Chapman—was an American trailblazer in the early 1800s. He traveled from place to place in the frontier states of Ohio and Indiana, establishing tree nurseries and selling the seedlings to settlers as they traveled west. Johnny cared deeply about animals and nature. He was friends with everyone living on the frontier—selling seeds and seedlings, pitching in with chores, and sharing news and adventurous stories. He inspired people with his wisdom and goodwill and helped create a countryside filled with fruit trees. The circular motifs used on several pages enrich the charming text.

The Last Puppy

By Frank Asch. Illustrated by the author. Prentice-Hall, 1980.

The youngest puppy is last to eat from Momma and sleep in the doghouse. He predicts that he'll be last to find an owner. He sabotages his efforts by being anxious and overexcited and by making mistakes! "Take me, take me!" barks the last puppy, but he comes across as too noisy. He inadvertently pushes a lady backward into a bowl of milk by jumping on her. He bites a man's nose when he plays too rough. Finally, the last puppy is picked up by a little boy. The puppy gently licks the boy's face, and the boy exclaims, "You are my first puppy."

Wilfrid Gordon McDonald Partridge

By Mem Fox. Illustrated by Julie Vivas. Kane/Miller, 1984.

From time to time an Alzheimer's or dementia patient may experience a lucid moment and enjoy the vitality of rich memories. Young Wilfrid lives next to a retirement home and wants to help Miss Nancy, who has lost her memory. Illustrated in dynamic watercolors, the story unfolds as Wilfrid tries to understand the concept of memory through the explanations of the old folks—something that makes you laugh, something that makes you warm, something that is as precious as gold. He gathers objects that make him laugh, make him warm, and are as precious as gold to jog Miss Nancy's memory.

The Lion and the Mouse

Adapted and illustrated by Jerry Pinkney. Little, Brown, 2009.

Award-winning author and illustrator Jerry Pinkney won the 2010 Caldecott Medal for his wordless adaptation of the classic Aesop fable "The Lion and the Mouse." Pinkney's stunning watercolors impart the story of a lion who spares a mouse, who in turn saves the lion. A tiny mouse literally stumbles upon the king of the jungle. The lion offhandedly decides to let the mouse go instead of eating him. Later the mouse hears an angry roar and finds the lion caught in a hunter's net. Without hesitation the mouse chews the rope, setting the lion free. A lifelong friendship begins.

Tsunami!

By Kimiko Kajikawa. Illustrated by Ed Young. Philomel, 2009.

Sacrificing does not necessarily mean suffering. This lesson is demonstrated in a powerful story of goodwill, sacrifice, and gratitude. One morning Ojiisan senses that something is not quite right. He decides to stay on his farm on the hill and does not join his family for the village festival near the sea. An earthquake rumbles in the ocean. The people are unaware of the "monster wave" rushing toward their village. Ojiisan quickly sets fire to his fields of rice to create an emergency. The entire village runs to help him put out the fire. Ojiisan sacrifices his rice fields but saves the villagers.

Baby Baobab

By Cindy Robinson. Illustrated by the author. Jacana Media, 2009.

Robinson teaches the lesson of humility through this traditional African tale. She uses distinctive illustrations to tell the story of the baby baobab tree's penalty for being selfish and rude. Baby Baobab exclaims that he is too big and beautiful to help the buzzing bee or the hornbill bird or Mr. and Mrs. Bat. He drives away the caterpillar and monkey who live in his branches. The sun intervenes and turns the tree upside down, with its roots in the air and its branches in the ground. Baby Baobab has forever learned his lesson and begins treating his neighbors as friends.

The Story of Ferdinand, 75th Anniversary Edition

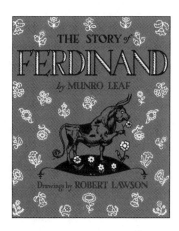

By Munro Leaf. Illustrated by Robert Lawson. Viking, 2011.

This classic and delightful story, first published by Viking in 1936, reveals the advantages of being quiet and gentle. As a young bull, Ferdinand discovers that he relishes quiet time under a cork tree and enjoys the scent of flowers. The other bulls growing up in the same pasture strive to be fast and rough and hope to be selected by five men in funny hats to fight in Madrid. One day Ferdinand sits on a bee, and the sting causes him to run fast, snort, and paw the ground. The five men carry *him* away to Madrid. When he enters the ring, however, he doesn't fight. Instead, he sees flowers and sits down quietly to savor their aroma.

Feelings

S A CHILD ABLE TO SIT STILL, PATIENTLY WAITING HIS OR HER turn? Does the child get along with others? These behaviors and interpersonal skills can be developed through exposure to storybooks that present characters grappling with how to acquire these capabilities. When children increase their emotional maturity—that is, the ability to experience and express their feelings in a positive way—they are better able to handle challenges. Some books in this section may be didactic; nevertheless they convey the essence of this topic's theme: helping children learn lessons of emotional control. Some books focus on identifying and naming feelings. We recommend not stopping there, but also sharing other books that help children learn to respond to and control their feelings. Parents and caregivers can find additional information about helping children with their feelings in John Gottman's *Raising an Emotionally Intelligent Child* (New York: Fireside, 1998) and at the Center for Social and Emotional Foundations of Learning, http://csefel.vanderbilt.edu.

Dorothea Lachner

Andrew's ANGRY Words

Illustrated by Thé Tjong-Khing

Andrew's Angry Words

By Dorothea Lachner. Illustrated by Thé Tjong-Khing. NorthSouth, 1995.

As soon as Andrew yells at his sister, he is sorry. It's too late, however, to stop the ripple effect of his bad mood, which touches his sister's friend, a poet, a motorcyclist, and a princess. Andrew's angry words are eventually tossed into the sea by a wise fruit vendor. The story then happily reverses, with a bouquet of nice words and a pleasant mood rippling back through the characters. Lachner presents a cautionary tale about the effect of emotions on others.

Knuffle Bunny: A Cautionary Tale

By Mo Willems. Illustrated by the author. Hyperion, 2004.

In this Caldecott honor book, Mo Willems presents a brilliant and hilarious story of Trixie's misadventure with her father at the laundromat. Trixie is too young to talk, and she becomes anxious and downright panicky when she cannot communicate—in words—that her stuffed animal is missing. Trixie's father doesn't understand the significance of the problem and downplays her feelings, a situation that children can relate to. All ends well, however, as Trixie blurts out her first words—"Knuffle Bunny"—when her friend is finally rescued. The colorful drawings of people over sepia-toned photographs are visually fun and appealing.

I Wish I Were a Butterfly

By James Howe. Illustrated by Ed Young. Harcourt Brace, 1987.

The littlest cricket in Swampswallow Pond is wallowing in self-pity. He can't shake the frog's remark that the cricket is the "ugliest creature he ever saw." Groaning, he says he wants to be a butterfly. The glowworm, the ladybug, the dragonfly, and the Old One, a wise spider, help teach the cricket not to be envious of others and to appreciate his own beauty. The artwork of Caldecott medalist Ed Young is stunning. The reader is immersed in the tall grasses around the pond, observing the action firsthand. Children will be more than pleased with the cricket's triumphant outcome.

Scaredy Squirrel

By Mélanie Watt. Illustrated by the author. Kids Can, 2006.

Scaredy Squirrel weighs the advantages of never leaving his tree—excellent view; lots of nuts; safe place; no killer bees, green Martians, or sharks. He has an emergency kit in case something unexpected happens, and he enjoys a routine of waking up, eating a nut, looking at the view, eating a nut, looking at the view, and going to sleep. He explores the disadvantages—same view, same nuts, and same old place. However, he makes no changes, until one day he is forced to jump to save his falling emergency kit. Something incredible happens—he starts to glide and becomes overjoyed, carefree, adventurous, and alive!

Mrs. Biddlebox

By Linda Smith. Illustrated by Marla Frazee. HarperCollins, 2002.

Don't let the gloomy illustrations darken your interest in this marvelous book about overcoming a grumpy mood. Mrs. Biddlebox wakes up on the wrong side of the bunk but determinedly decides to cook the rotten morning and turn it into cake! Her jaunty ponytail swings to and fro as she gets busy gathering up the gloom, plucking a filthy shadow from her skirt and adding it to the pot. After stirring and twirling the concoction, she hooks a ray of sun as the final ingredient. The day bakes "merrily" and turns out sweet.

No Such Thing

By Jackie French Koller. Illustrated by Betsy Lewin. Boyds Mills, 1997.

This playful tale with a delightful twist zeroes in on the common childhood fear of monsters under the bed. A boy on top of the bed and a monster under the bed are told by their mothers that there is "no such thing" as a monster under the bed . . . or a boy on top of the bed. The charming text and expressive illustrations will have adults and children laughing out loud, especially at the surprise ending.

Ten, Nine, Eight

By Molly Bang. Illustrated by the author. Greenwillow, 1983.
Reading storybooks at bedtime is a perfect way to help children establish a routine for quieting the emotions and going to sleep. Molly Bang's *Ten, Nine, Eight,* a Caldecott honor book, exudes reassurance during the bedtime routine. She makes counting down a gentle adventure: an odd number of shoes lined up by the bed, colorful buttons on a nightgown, sleepy eyes of dad and daughter, and a "big girl all ready for bed."

Spoon

By Amy Krouse Rosenthal. Illustrated by Scott Magoon. Disney-Hyperion, 2009.
Magoon's illustrations of Spoon and his family and friends are the perfect match for Rosenthal's pragmatic tale of learning to recognize, appreciate, and value one's own strengths and those of others. Young Spoon feels jealous of the things his friends can do that he cannot. Knife can cut and spread. Fork can go outside and help on the grill. Spoon's parents guide him to appreciate his special abilities, such as diving headfirst into a bowl of ice cream and relaxing in a hot cup of tea. Spoon is rejuvenated and enjoys life again.

Grumpy Bird

By Jeremy Tankard. Illustrated by the author. Scholastic Press, 2007.
Are you looking for a cure for grumpiness? Tankard's spot-on depiction of this bad-tempered feathered friend's ability to transform a potentially bad day into a good day will charm adults and children alike. To change his mood, Grumpy Bird gets busy by taking a walk. Children will enjoy seeing how Grumpy Bird's friends ignore his foul mood and have fun imitating him on his walk. The appealing illustrations are simple and colorful.

Stalling

By Alan Katz. Illustrated by Elwood H. Smith. Margaret K. McElderry, 2010.
Mom and Dad say it's time to go to sleep. Dan says he doesn't have time for counting sheep. He dashes off to hunt, dance, magnify, stack blocks, smell socks, play hallway soccer, part his hair, inflate a whale, visit the Nile,

hide stuff in his dresser drawers, check his height, and "walkie-talkie with Milwaukee." *Stalling* will teach children more than fifty marvelous ways to postpone bedtime. It's hilarious! It's exhausting! The mixture of illustration and photography perfectly fits Dan's energetic bedtime frolic.

Bedtime for Frances

By Russell Hoban. Illustrated by Garth Williams. Harper, 1960.

Frances, the little badger, first delays bedtime with silly antics and then imagines scary tigers, giants, and spiders as she tries to fall asleep. This 1960 original Frances book is nearly perfect in showing a child's overly active imagination and how parents can help a child learn to control fear. Father and Mother display patience, kindness, love, and humor as they foster emotional control. Williams's illustrations are an excellent depiction—whether in the original black-and-white or the later colorized version—of this warm and loving story of growing up a day at a time.

Three Little Kittens: A Folk Tale Classic

Adapted and illustrated by Paul Galdone. Houghton Mifflin Harcourt, 2011.

Paul Galdone's retelling of this classic tale was released in a 2011 edition. Children will relate to the kittens as they grapple with the lesson of consequences: if you lose or soil your mittens, "you shall have no pie." The lively watercolor illustrations and clear text enhance this fun nursery rhyme.

Little Hoot

By Amy Krouse Rosenthal. Illustrated by Jen Corace. Chronicle, 2008.

Little Hoot's friends can go to bed early, so why can't he? Why is he the only one who has to stay up late and play? Little Hoot is a happy young owl who enjoys going to school and playing with his forest friends. He does not mind when Mama Owl tells him it's time to practice important skills owls need to know, such as pondering and staring. However, when it comes to bedtime, Little Hoot does not like the sensible owl tradition of staying up late. Children will hoot and giggle their way to sleep.

The Tale of Peter Rabbit

By Beatrix Potter. Illustrated by the author. Warne, 2002.

Peter Rabbit is an adventurous bunny, but while exploring Mr. McGregor's garden, a forbidden place, he gets into trouble and becomes very frightened. Beatrix Potter was one of our great storytellers and artists. This timeless story, originally published in 1902, captures a range of emotions, including excitement, discouragement, and fright. The book brilliantly presents—through an engaging story and beautiful illustrations—a safe way for children to see the dangerous consequences of not following a parent's rule.

Goodnight Moon

By Margaret Wise Brown. Illustrated by Clement Hurd. Harper, 1947.

Reading this 1947 classic aloud at bedtime calms the emotions. It can successfully distract young children from any worried thoughts they may have when falling asleep. The book takes a child through a young rabbit's bedtime ritual of saying "goodnight" to every object in sight. The poetic beauty of the text and the routine of finding the items in the splendid illustrations gently lull a child to sleep.

Little Miss Sunshine

By Roger Hargreaves. Illustrated by the author. Price, Stern, Sloan, reprint edition, 2011.

Little Miss Sunshine shines as one of the first in the English series of forty-two endearing and sensible Little Miss books. Originally published in 1981, ten years after the Mr. Men series began, the book focuses on encouraging all of us to cultivate the ability to smile, chuckle, giggle, and laugh. Little Miss Sunshine boldly delivers a royal message to the king of Miseryland that no matter what is occurring around us, we can always find and use these inner resources. Little Miss was popularized as a television show.

Mr. Happy

By Roger Hargreaves. Illustrated by the author. Price, Stern, Sloan, reprint edition, 2011.

Mr. Happy stands out in this English series of forty-nine remarkable Mr. Men books. Originally published in 1971, this little book shouts a big message: if you feel miserable, you have the choice to influence your outlook on life and change your mood. Mr. Happy invites Mr. Miserable to his cottage in Happyland. There, Mr. Miserable learns it's just as easy to turn his frown into a smile as it is to stay miserable. The simple drawings are colorful, clean, and uplifting. Mr. Men was popularized as a television show.

Baby Faces (a board book)

By Margaret Miller. Photographs by the author. Little Simon, 2009.
Babies enjoy songs, rhymes, and photos of other babies. Adorable close-up photos of baby faces make this a winning board book for babies and toddlers. Children will learn to identify feelings such as sad—"boo hoo"—and happy—"yippee." A caring adult will have fun expressing emotions with baby.

Owen

By Kevin Henkes. Illustrated by the author. Greenwillow, 1993.
One day Mrs. Tweezers, the next-door neighbor, suggests that Owen is getting too old to be attached to his blanket, Fuzzy. Owen's parents try several tricks, such as replacing Fuzzy with a "positively perfect, especially terrific big-boy gift," dipping a corner of the blanket into vinegar, and just saying no. Finally, Owen's mother cuts, sews, and snips Fuzzy into new handkerchiefs—one for each day! This Caldecott honor book will delight children and parents alike.

Shy Charles

By Rosemary Wells. Illustrated by the author. Dial, 1988.

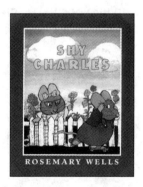

What better way to help timid children than to give them a shy hero? Parents and children will relate to the frustrations of shy Charles, the bunny. At the end of the day, Charles's quiet confidence and competence during a crisis save Mrs. Block, the babysitter. Award-winning Wells uses pleasing illustrations and takes a cheerful approach to this common childhood experience. The story gently nudges children to overcome their shyness by focusing on their strengths.

Sheila Rae, the Brave

By Kevin Henkes. Illustrated by the author. Greenwillow, 1987.
Sheila Rae is not frightened of anything, including walking backward with her eyes closed, until she gets lost. Her "scaredy-cat" sister, Louise, helps her find the way home. Henkes teaches children that as they learn and

grow, it is okay sometimes to be shy and afraid. Often it is by confronting the feelings of shyness and fear that we develop courage and confidence. The book provides the opportunity for adults to cope with the complexity of helping children feel protected while also fostering independence.

Where the Wild Things Are

By Maurice Sendak. Illustrated by the author. Harper and Row, 1988.
Through a wild, delightful adventure, award-winning Sendak encourages children to safely use their imaginations to control emotions and manage their thoughts. This 1964 Caldecott winner tells the story of mischievous Max, who is sent to bed without supper. Max fantasizes about the land of the Wild Things—personifications of frustration, anger, and loneliness. Max uses his creativity to confront the wild things in his imagination. He successfully leaves them behind as he returns to his room—to the love of his family—and finds a warm supper on a tray.

The Magic Hat

By Mem Fox. Illustrated by Tricia Tusa. Harcourt, 2002.
Fox and Tusa team up in this joyful story of a magical hat that turns a curmudgeon into a toad, a fruit-stand owner into a baboon, and a sleepy old man into a bear. We follow the fabulous hat as it spins through the air from one innocent bystander to the next. The warm, cartoonlike artwork will appeal to children's sense of fun and playfulness. A surprise ending closes this delightful romp through the land of silliness.

Wemberly Worried

By Kevin Henkes. Illustrated by the author. Greenwillow, 2000.
Whether children are occasional or frequent worriers, they will benefit from this gentle yet powerful story. Wemberly, a shy mouse, has a tendency to worry about the crack in the living room wall, the chains on the swing in the playground, whether her friends will come to her birthday party, and even the tree in the yard. With the help of Mrs. Peachum and a special classmate, Wemberly learns to control her anxiety and have fun as she starts nursery school.

Bawk and Roll

By Tammi Sauer. Illustrated by Dan Santat. Sterling, 2012.
Marge and Lola, the Chicken Dancers, are thrilled to be selected to go on tour with Elvis Poultry. They've got style. They've got rhythm. However, they soon discover they also have stage fright! What should they do? Elvis tells them to chill. They try calming their jitters by painting, meditating, knitting, and taking long, hot baths. They try picturing the crowd in tightie whities. Nothing works. Finally they realize that they are missing their friends from the barnyard back home. A busload of familiar faces shows up and cheers them on. Marge and Lola's performance is top-notch and inspires Elvis to come up with a new song: "Blue Mooooooo"!

When Fuzzy Was Afraid of Losing His Mother

By Inger Maier. Illustrated by Jennifer Candon. Magination, 2005.
In this instructive and practical picture book about Fuzzy the Little Sheep, Maier, a clinical psychologist, offers tips for dealing with separation. When Fuzzy's mother goes out for apples, Fuzzy becomes immobilized and lets his imagination run away with him. His mother invents several ways for Fuzzy to focus his thoughts and attention whenever she is running errands. In time, he is successful in controlling his fear. Fuzzy enjoys racing with his friends and jumping in puddles even though his mother is away.

When Lizzy Was Afraid of Trying New Things

By Inger Maier. Illustrated by Jennifer Candon. Magination, 2005.
Lizzy the sheep is crippled with shyness and doesn't have much fun. Fuzzy comes up with a brilliant idea to help his sister gain self-assurance. Starting with easy activities, such as picking a dandelion, Lizzy earns a rock for every time she tries doing something new. She even says hello to big, smart Cousin Curley and can walk her back legs up the apple tree without falling. By the end of the story she exudes confidence and enjoys life! The good humor of the text, the lively illustrations, and the outstanding message can help bolster a shy child to try new things.

Mouse Was Mad

By Linda Urban. Illustrated by Henry Cole. Harcourt, 2009.
After trying several methods of managing his anger, Mouse discovers that by standing very still, he can control his anger and feel bet-

ter. Bear, who stomps when mad, Bobcat, who screams, and other animal friends are impressed and inspired by Mouse's method. The story offers children a splendid example of learning self-regulation and getting on with the business of enjoying life. Award-winning Cole has created the perfect illustrations to fit the text.

The Grouchy Ladybug

By Eric Carle. Illustrated by the author. T. Y. Crowell, 1977.
In this beautifully illustrated book, award-winning Carle shares a universal lesson about the pointlessness of being grouchy. The cantankerous ladybug tries to pick a fight, but she learns to settle herself down and become her better, more amiable self. The story can be used to discuss the benefits of controlling moods and using polite manners. An additional, delightful feature is the book's lessons about comparative size and telling time.

Bear Feels Scared

By Karma Wilson. Illustrated by Jane Chapman. Margaret K. McElderry, 2008.
Wilson shares a reassuring story in *Bear Feels Scared*. Bear goes for a walk in the woods, but he cannot find his way back home. A storm begins, and Bear feels scared and all alone. Before long, his woodland friends set out to search for him and bring him home safe and sound. Children will enjoy the rhyme, repetition, and charming illustrations of this comforting tale. This book provides the opportunity to help children deal with the fear of getting lost and has the added benefit of illustrating how those who care about you can help you feel safe.

I Can Share (a lift-the-flap book)

By Karen Katz. Illustrated by the author. Grosset and Dunlap, 2004.
Katz guides young children in this excellent book on learning to share. Each situation begins with the common reaction of children when faced with a request to share and then turns into a lesson on being flexible and learning to share. You may not ride my bike, but maybe . . . you can ride it with me. You can't have my new doll, but maybe . . . you can play with *this* doll. You can't play with my friend, but maybe . . . we can all play together. The cheerful illustrations complement the upbeat message.

Hands Are Not for Hitting

By Martine Agassi. Illustrated by Marieka Heinlen. Free Spirit, 2000.
Hands are for playing, learning, asking questions, counting, painting, clapping, doing, building, helping, and brushing your teeth, but they are not for hitting or pushing. Agassi has created an effective tool for teaching self-control.

Listening Time

By Elizabeth Verdick. Illustrated by Marieka Heinlen. Free Spirit, 2008.
For adults and children alike, active listening skills can enhance productivity and improve relationships. *Listening Time* gently teaches very young children to put away their giggles and wiggles because listening works best when you are "calm and still." The charming artwork advances the rhyming and spare text. A "listening tips" page at the end of the book encourages parents and caregivers to be role models and to help their child practice these skills using lighthearted reminders and praise.

Calm-Down Time (a board book)

By Elizabeth Verdick. Illustrated by Marieka Heinlen. Free Spirit, 2010.
"One, two, three . . . I'm taking care of me." This board book offers parents and young children a tool for calming the emotions. Verdick suggests several methods—including having a special quiet place or taking a deep breath or getting hugs from a caring adult—to help children gain composure and feel like new. This well-written book has garnered several awards, including *Creative Child* magazine's 2011 Preferred Choice Award.

No Biting! (a lift-the-flap book)

By Karen Katz. Illustrated by the author. Grosset and Dunlap, 2002.
Toddlers may go through a period of biting others. Katz addresses not only biting but also pushing, hitting, kicking, and spitting. Each negative behavior is countered with a positive alternative: bite apples and not friends, kick balls and not dogs, and spit when brushing your teeth and not

while playing with your brother. This simple but effective handbook can launch a child's journey to discover self-discipline.

Where's My Teddy?

By Jez Alborough. Illustrated by the author. Candlewick, 1992.
Alborough offers the opportunity for children to experience fears within the safety of a picture book. Eddie journeys into the woods to look for his lost teddy bear. He soon discovers a gigantic teddy bear and hears a bear crying nearby. After startling each other and grabbing the right teddy, Eddie and the bear each make their way back home safe and sound. Fabulous watercolors portray the scary (but not too scary) forest.

Go Away, Big Green Monster!

By Ed Emberley. Illustrated by the author. Little, Brown, 1992.
Caldecott medalist Emberley has designed a brilliant tool for children to dissolve their imagined scary monsters into nothingness. Many children from time to time create fantastic giants or nighttime monsters or mysterious cowboys hiding in the closet or under the bed. With each turn of the page, this die-cut book slowly creates a big green monster with sharp white teeth. Then, as you continue to turn the pages, the process reverses, and the monster disappears completely. Children can learn an effective way to control their anxious feelings and runaway thoughts while enjoying this colorful, fun book.

The I'm Not Scared Book

By Todd Parr. Illustrated by the author. Little, Brown, 2011.
Best-selling author Parr reassures anxious children through a playful series of paired scary situations and solutions. It may be scary to make a mistake, but it's not scary to know I did my best. It may be scary when there is a family argument, but it's not scary when everyone hugs and says, "I'm sorry." The charming and simple illustrations grab a young child's attention. The book provides the opportunity for adults and children to talk about controlling fear and anxiety.

How Are You Peeling? Foods with Moods

By Saxton Freymann and Joost Elffers. Illustrated by Saxton Freymann. Arthur A. Levine, 1999.
Happy? Sad? Blue? Bad? Wonderfully imaginative faces expressing a variety of emotions are carved from fruits and vegetables and photographed

against brightly colored backgrounds. Simple rhyming text allows exploration of personal feelings and suggests possible answers: Frustrated? Amused? Surprised? Confused? *How Are You Peeling?* is a great resource for exploring the many words we have to express human feeling and emotion. It offers an opportunity to discuss the facial features that signal feelings. Readers will enjoy examining the charming pictures, which may inspire children to create their own food art.

Franklin in the Dark
By Paulette Bourgeois. Illustrated by Brenda Clark. Kids Can, 1986.
This tale in the classic Franklin series offers a forum for adults and children to discuss what scares them and how to minimize their fears. Franklin the turtle is afraid to sleep in his shell at night. He discovers that his friends are afraid of something too. The lion is fearful of loud noises. The duck is afraid to swim in deep water. The wren is frightened of flying too high. Each friend has found a way to overcome his or her fear. Franklin realizes that he, too, can be brave and figure out a solution—which he does!

The Pout-Pout Fish
By Deborah Diesen. Illustrated by Dan Hanna. Farrar Straus Giroux, 2008.
Are you a "pout-pout" fish or a "kiss-kiss" fish? That's the question! Diesen depicts the transformation of grumpy Mr. Fish into a cheerful friend who spreads goodwill to all. Hanna's lighthearted illustrations perfectly match the rhyming rhythm of the text. The story can help change a gloomy mood into a bright disposition.

The Pout-Pout Fish in the Big-Big Dark
By Deborah Diesen. Illustrated by Dan Hanna. Farrar Straus Giroux, 2010.
Diesen and Hanna team up once again to tell a radiant story of how Mr. Fish of *The Pout-Pout Fish* conquers his fear of the dark and helps Ms. Clam find her lost pearl. Mr. Fish musters a little courage and relies on his friends to overcome his anxious feelings. He bravely swims into the deepest and darkest part of the ocean to retrieve the lost pearl and save the day.

Thunder Cake
By Patricia Polacco. Illustrated by the author. Philomel, 1990.
Polacco retells her childhood experience of overcoming her fear of thunder under the loving guidance and ingenuity of her grandma—her Babushka. Thunder is heard in the distance. Grandma steadies her granddaughter's

fear by distracting the little girl with the project of baking a "thunder cake." Each step of the baking process coincides with the thunderstorm traveling closer to the farmhouse. Grandma keeps them focused on the task at hand. Finally, the cake is served as it starts to rain. The cake recipe in the back of the book sounds delicious!

When I Care about Others

By Cornelia Maude Spelman. Illustrated by Kathy Parkinson. Albert Whitman, 2002.

One of the oldest sayings common to cultures, religions, and philosophies around the world is "Do unto others as you would have them do unto you." Spelman presents an appropriate version of this important rule for young children. Parkinson's warm illustrations of a bear family and their everyday activities as they connect with others make this book a winner for any public or home library. A note to parents and teachers offers useful tips on empathy.

Curiosity and Exploring the World

A S A FOUR-YEAR-OLD READY TO WALK A FEW BLOCKS ALONE TO Grandmother's house? For some children, depending on the circumstances, this scenario would be a reasonable risk; for others, it would not. The world is a very large place. It does contain some fearsome things, but it also contains many wonderful things for children to explore. The following titles provide opportunities for parents and caregivers to help children grow up confident, optimistic, and full of vitality. After all, a child can hold Mommy's hand for only so long before his or her curiosity must be satisfied.

Dali and the Path of Dreams

By Anna Obiols. Illustrated by Joan Subirana. Frances Lincoln, 2004.
This brilliant story of Salvador Dali's dreamy childhood is entertaining, educational, and enlightening. Young Dali finds a key on the beach, and thus begins an adventure of discovery—long-legged elephants, a cook tossing clocks like a pizza pie, a bread-headed cyclist, a lady with butterfly wings, a snail tamer, and a tower with mysterious drawers and doors.

Each person and object settles down to live in a drawer. When Dali grows up he uses his magical key to unlock the drawer and paint all the peculiar and wonderful people and objects of his childhood dreams. The delightful illustrations emulate Dali's paintings.

Henry Hikes to Fitchburg

By D. B. Johnson. Illustrated by the author. Houghton Mifflin, 2000.
This adorable story of Henry Thoreau was inspired by the *Walden* passage about traveling to Fitchburg. If you go by train, as Henry's friend learns, you need to earn money. As Henry chooses, you can start off right away on foot. Henry's friend earns ten cents by filling Mrs. Alcott's woodbox, while Henry hops from rock to rock across the river. The friend sweeps the post office for five cents. Henry carves a walking stick. The friend pulls Mr. Hawthorne's garden weeds and moves bookcases in Mr. Emerson's study, while Henry stops to pick ferns and flowers to press in a book, swims in a pond, and climbs a tree. Although the train is faster, Henry's walk is richer.

Odd Boy Out: Young Albert Einstein

By Don Brown. Illustrated by the author. Houghton Mifflin, 2004.
Exploring the mysteries of a compass, studying the shapes in a geometry book, and learning to play Mozart on the violin catapulted young Einstein into higher realms of thinking, problem solving, and discovery. His peculiar and often amusing personality traits make it easy for children to relate to this future Nobel Prize winner. Brown's biography encourages us all to be curious about and in awe of life's wonders. Amazingly, Einstein pondered physics—proving that atoms exist and designing the theories of light and relativity—in his spare time while fulfilling his obligations as a new husband, father, and patent office worker.

Now and Ben:
The Modern Inventions of Benjamin Franklin

By Gene Barretta. Illustrated by the author. Henry Holt, 2006.
Can you imagine a world without the public library, the odometer, the fire department, or bifocal glasses? These are a few examples of how Benjamin Franklin applied his curiosity and imagination to create pragmatic inventions and community improvements. Barretta's innovative format shows the modern services and amenities on one page of the spread and captures Ben's original idea on the other page of the spread. The relaxed and cheer-

ful illustrations depict the quirkiness and brilliance of this ever-curious founding father.

Neo Leo: The Ageless Ideas of Leonardo da Vinci

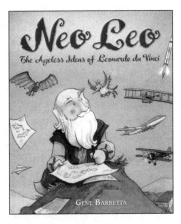

By Gene Barretta. Illustrated by the author. Henry Holt, 2009.

How can you inspire young children to be inventive? One delightful way is to read, share, and help them memorize this exciting picture book about Leonardo da Vinci. Similar in scope and style to Barretta's *Now and Ben* about Benjamin Franklin, *Neo Leo* demonstrates curiosity and innovative thinking at its best. Leonardo designed and put down on paper thousands of ideas, diagrams, and experiments. Although not all practical then or now, many of his devices prove his forward-looking brilliance—a man-powered aircraft, scuba gear, vortex formation in the blood, steam power, a self-propelled cart, and a parachute.

Balloons over Broadway: The True Story of the Puppeteer of Macy's Parade

By Melissa Sweet. Illustrated by the author. Houghton Mifflin, 2011.

As a child Tony Sarg was fascinated by "how to make things move." He designed a pulley mechanism to open the chicken coop door so that he could stay in bed at 6:30 a.m. but still feed the chickens. Sarg turned his hobby into a career in puppetry in New York City. He eventually designed a mechanical puppet parade using pulleys in Macy's window display. When Thanksgiving Day parade organizers realized that lions and tigers often frighten children, Macy's asked Sarg to think of "something spectacular" for the parade. Curiosity led Sarg to design the famous helium balloon puppets controlled by rope handlers.

The Complete Adventures of Curious George

Written and illustrated by Margret and H. A. Rey. Houghton Mifflin Harcourt, 2010.

What better hero than Curious George, the good little monkey? He delights children when his curiosity creates hilarious predicaments, such as when he wonders whether the ostrich would eat a bugle. He has a conscience when he's made a mistake and is "terribly sorry." He makes amends by helping to solve problems—for example, he musters courage in order to save a baby bear in trouble. This seventieth-anniversary edition contains all seven original tales by the Reys.

Max's Castle

By Kate Banks. Illustrated by Boris Kulikov. Farrar Straus Giroux, 2011.
Get ready for a fast-paced romp, as Max exercises his curiosity with just a set of alphabet letter blocks, a box of toys, and a dinosaur skeleton. His older brothers ask to join the fun as Max creates a castle filled with adventure. Max uses the letters on the blocks to play with words as he designs each masterpiece—WALLS, HALLS, MOAT, and BOAT. He encounters PIRATES and turns them into RAT PIES and turns a SWORD into WORDS. When the boys encounter a CATASTROPHE, they turn the letters around looking for a way out, finding HOPE and eventually escaping the dungeon. The expressive illustrations burst with energy.

Just One Bite

By Lola M. Schaefer. Illustrated by Geoff Waring. Chronicle, 2010.
How much can a bear or parrot or butterfly eat in just one bite? Award-winning Schaefer has posed this question about eleven animals. She teams with Waring to produce an intriguing narrative nonfiction book. Each animal and each bite are charmingly illustrated in life size. The 12-by-12-inch dimensions of the book enable the face of a giraffe to fit on a two-page spread. For the larger animals, such as the elephant and sperm whale, the pages magically fold out. Children will be fascinated and delighted with each bite!

A Penguin Story

By Antoinette Portis. Illustrated by the author. HarperCollins, 2009.
Edna's life is made up of three colors: white for the ice, black for night, and blue for the ocean. She appreciates these colors but wonders whether there is "something else." Her curiosity is set in motion. She asks questions, ponders the answers, and searches the world around her. Coming

upon a camp of scientists, she delights in the orange color of their parkas and tents. The neat and cheerful illustrations capture the simplicity and serenity of Antarctica and convey Portis's humor.

The Tale of Peter Rabbit

By Beatrix Potter. Illustrated by the author. Warne, 2002.
Peter Rabbit is an adventurous bunny, but while exploring Mr. McGregor's garden, a forbidden place, he gets into trouble and becomes very frightened. Beatrix Potter was one of our great storytellers and artists. This timeless story, originally published in 1902, captures a range of emotions, including excitement, discouragement, and fright. The book brilliantly presents—through an engaging story and beautiful illustrations—a safe way for children to see the dangerous consequences of not following a parent's rule.

Once upon a Dragon: Stranger Safety for Kids (and Dragons)

By Jean E. Pendziwol. Illustrated by Martine Gourbault. Kids Can, 2006.
A little girl protects her dragon buddy as they romp around inside her fairy-tale book. They thwart danger as they encounter a strange wolf, an evil queen, a sly fox, and others in familiar stories, such as Little Red Riding Hood. The girl safeguards the dragon again and again, pointing out the potential pitfalls of his choices. The rhyme and rhythm of the text are delightful: the wrong way is "lonely and dark" and will not lead them "back to the park." The good-humored illustrations capture a positive tone, helping young children grasp safety rules without inciting undue anxiety.

I Can Be Safe: A First Look at Safety

By Pat Thomas. Illustrated by Lesley Harker. Barron's Educational Series, 2003.
How can children learn to look after themselves as they grow up? This book can be a friendly tool for helping children understand "what is safe and what is not." Thomas and Harker have captured the essence of this topic: be cautious, but enjoy life.

Be Careful and Stay Safe

By Cheri J. Meiners. Illustrated by Meredith Johnson. Free Spirit, 2007.
The text and illustrations in this upbeat and pragmatic lesson book come straight to the point: it's important to make new friends, and it's important

to talk with strangers only when a trusted grown-up is present. Parents can prompt children to think about each lesson with a question or two from a section in the back of the book called "Ways to Reinforce the Ideas." Games and other activity suggestions, such as "Staying Safe at Home and School," can inspire parents to establish basic safety rules without causing anxiety in their children.

The Berenstain Bears Learn about Strangers

Written and illustrated by Stan and Jan Berenstain. Random House, 1985.
This story balances how young children should think about strangers. After hearing the newspaper story about cub-napping, Sister's perspective is warped by fear. Even butterflies seem "mean and scary to Sister." After a lesson from Mama about being careful—but not paranoid—because of a few "bad apples," Sister is able to be her usual friendly self. Another lesson unfolds as Brother allows his enthusiasm for toy airplanes to break the rule about strangers, even though the stranger was probably not a bad apple. A list of the bears' rules complement the story.

Not Everyone Is Nice:
Helping Children Learn Caution with Strangers

By Frederick Alimonti and Ann Tedesco. Illustrated by Erik DePrince and Jessica Volinski. New Horizon, 2003.
Many parents will appreciate this story as a discussion starter for teaching their children not to talk to strangers. Kathy is puzzled during a conversation with a stranger as she waits for her mother to pick her up after school. The encounter and her parents' response to it can help children learn to follow basic rules about dealing with strangers. The narrative, dialogue, and illustrations set the right tone for helping most young children to understand safety issues without provoking fear.

Safety at the Swimming Pool

By Lucia Raatma. Illustrated with photographs. Bridgestone, 1999.
High-quality photographs help depict basic pool safety tips in this useful book. Raatma offers clear guidelines to help families enjoy the benefits and fun of swimming. For example, she encourages children to get out of the pool if they are "cold or tired." Higher-level words, such as *emergency* and *sunscreen*, are explained at the bottom of the page. A glossary, a hands-on activity, and an index complete the text.

Smoky Night

By Eve Bunting. Illustrated by David Diaz. Harcourt Brace, 1994.

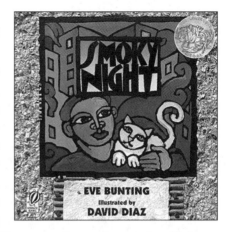

This 1995 Caldecott winner stresses the need for children to understand why parents make rules and why it is important to follow those rules. Bunting emphasizes that parents make rules because they care about their children and want to keep them safe. She demonstrates how Daniel obeys his mother during each stage of the Los Angeles riot of the early 1990s. For example, as the smoke thickens, Daniel is instructed to put on his shoes: "Hurry!" The story within the story involves two lost cats who don't get along until they are brought together during the riot. It reminds everyone that life is better if we find common ground and can learn to cooperate.

New Baby

WHEN A NEW BABY JOINS A HOUSEHOLD, IT IS A joyous time. Older siblings usually share in this excitement—but may also have concerns. Attention from Mom and Dad may be in short supply. A child may doubt if there's enough love to go around. Daily routines may be interrupted. These concerns may be alleviated through open discussions that provide an understanding about the real, but temporary, nature of the family's disruptions. Children can then form accurate expectations of their new sibling and any changes that he or she may bring.

Books vary in their approach to the topic. Some focus on older siblings working through their difficult emotions. Some feature solely the positive aspects of the joyous event. And some just present straightforward information.

Lola Reads to Leo

By Anna McQuinn. Illustrated by Rosalind Beardshaw. Charlesbridge, 2012.
Lola, an African American girl, gets a baby brother named Leo. Being a big sister takes work. Lola helps her mommy and daddy take care of Leo by reading him stories when he is eating, crying, and taking a bath. She also helps by giving some of her books to Leo and chooses a perfect soft book for his crib. Everyone is busier because of the baby, but Mommy and Daddy still have time to read Lola a story at the end of the day. The colorful illustrations and simple text focus on the positive aspects of getting a new baby.

Baby Baby Blah Blah Blah!

By Jonathan Shipton. Illustrated by Francesca Chessa. Holiday House, 2009.
Emily makes a list about the upcoming baby. She shares the list with her parents, starting with why a baby is good and including "you can play pat-a-cake" and "you can tickle it to bits." But Emily's list also includes negatives—the baby only dribbles and cries. She then complains that when the baby comes, it will be all "baby goo goo" and "baby blah blah blah." To ease Emily's concern, her dad tells her about when she was a baby and reinforces that Mom and Dad will always love her. The large, colorful illustrations add to the humorous tone.

Babies Don't Eat Pizza

By Dianne Danzig. Illustrated by Debbie Tilley. Dutton, 2009.
Speaking to the early-elementary-age child, this book provides information about babies, such as what it's like for them prior to birth (squishy), how they are delivered (through an opening between Mom's legs), and what they like to eat (not pizza). Danzig offers suggestions about how siblings can help with the baby's caretaking. In the end she reminds children that they are unique and that their parents will always love them just as they are. Child-friendly illustrations include babies of various ages and ethnicities. A final page provides additional transition ideas for the parent or caregiver.

How to Be a Baby, by Me the Big Sister

By Sally Lloyd-Jones. Illustrated by Sue Heap. Schwartz and Wade, 2007.
A big sister tells her new sibling what it is like to be a baby. Using clever text and silly illustrations, Lloyd-Jones lovingly details the ways in which

being a big kid is superior. Things a baby cannot do include reading books (they eat them instead), singing songs, and eating pizza. Also, babies do not know how old they are, where they live, or even whether they are a girl or a boy. Babies don't have good manners, either. However, the sister realizes that babies are fun and that they will grow up to become good friends.

Back into Mommy's Tummy

By Thierry Robberecht. Illustrated by Philippe Goossens. Clarion, 2005.
Offering a unique angle on jealousy of an unborn sibling, this story is delightful and silly. On her fifth birthday, a little girl asks to go back into her pregnant mom's tummy so that her mom will think about her more often. Trying to convince her mom, she points out the perks of returning, which are comically illustrated. When her friends arrive for her birthday party, she realizes she would not be able to participate in her birthday festivities if she were in a tummy. She is comforted when her mom reassures her that she loves both her children equally.

There's Going to Be a Baby

By John Burningham. Illustrated by Helen Oxenbury. Candlewick, 2010.
A preschool-age boy asks his mother many questions about his soon-to-be-born sibling. His mother helps him imagine some of the things the baby may grow up to be: a chef, zookeeper, painter, or sailor. These discussions take place throughout her pregnancy, and illustrations show the passage of time through the changing weather and her expanding belly. At the beginning of the mother's pregnancy, the boy is apprehensive about the baby, asking for it to go away, but when the baby arrives, he announces, "The baby will be our baby. We're going to love the baby, aren't we?"

When the World Was Waiting for You

By Gillian Shields. Illustrated by Anna Currey. Bloomsbury, 2011.
A rabbit family plans for the arrival of their new baby by making its nursery cozy and setting out presents. The brothers and sisters are excited about the baby's arrival. "Will it be soon?" one asks. Finally the big day comes,

and the baby rabbit is born. Everyone is so happy. The new baby gets many visitors: Granny, Grandpa, Cousin Polly, Uncle John, and Auntie Molly. They all want to help the rabbit family celebrate. The striking and charming watercolor illustrations, along with rhyming text, help to convey the joys and pleasures of bringing a new baby into the world.

Not Yet, Rose
By Susanna Leonard Hill. Illustrated by Nicole Rutten. Eerdmans, 2009.
Rose, a little hamster, has changing emotions about becoming a big sister. On Monday, she is thrilled and wants a new sister. But she considers that a sister could be too much like her. On Tuesday, she decides that a brother would be better. As the week goes on, Rose begins to question her parents on their decision to have a new baby—after all, "You've already got me." Finally, her baby brother arrives, and Rose visits him in the hospital. She holds him, and he holds her hand. It is a good feeling, and Rose is happy to be a sister.

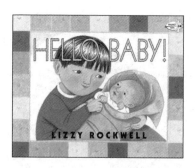

Hello Baby!
By Lizzy Rockwell. Illustrated by the author. Crown, 1999.
A young boy awaits his new sister, and he hears her heartbeat at his mommy's routine doctor exam. In the office, they see a gestation-period chart that describes fertilization, cell splitting, and body-part formation. Soon the big day arrives, and Eliza is born. The boy explains that Eliza drinks breast milk, the perfect food for a baby. He also helps his daddy give Eliza a sponge bath, and they wipe around the black scab that will peel and reveal a belly button. When Eliza begins to cry, her big brother knows just the trick to sooth his new sister.

Big Sister Now: A Story about Me and Our New Baby
By Annette Sheldon. Illustrated by Karen Maizel. Magination, 2006.
Kate used to feel warm and safe being the baby of the house. But now her brother, Daniel, has arrived, and she is assuming the role of big sister. Kate has to learn to be patient while Mommy and Daddy take care of Daniel,

but this does not come easily or without mishap. Through the process, however, Kate finds that being more independent makes her feel big, as well as warm and safe. Humorous illustrations help express the pains and joys of the new-baby transition. The book concludes with parenting tips for before and after the new baby arrives.

But I Wanted a Baby Brother!

By Kate Feiffer. Illustrated by Diane Goode. Simon and Schuster, 2010.
Oliver was excited to be getting a new brother. However, by "mistake" his parents came home with Julie, a new baby sister. Oliver sets off to exchange Julie for a baby boy. He finds that other babies can cry all day long. Julie doesn't cry very often. He also finds that other babies don't sleep through the night, and they keep the family awake. Julie sleeps all night. For over a year, Oliver searches with his dog for the perfect baby brother, but finally realizes how much he loves his baby sister. The cartoon-style illustrations enhance the humor of the story.

Julius, the Baby of the World

By Kevin Henkes. Illustrated by the author. Greenwillow, 1990.
Everything changes for Lilly the mouse when her brother is born. She hates him and gives him trouble. Although Lilly's parents say Julius is "the baby of the world," Lilly deems him "disgusting" and looks forward to the day when he is gone. But Lilly's parents inform her that Julius isn't going anywhere. Lilly continues her bad behavior by trying to pester and frighten her brother and spends extra time in her "uncooperative chair." But when Lilly's cousin, Garland, has his own nasty words about Julius, Lilly comes to her brother's defense. She declares him to be "the baby of the world."

Pecan Pie Baby

By Jacqueline Woodson. Illustrated by Sophie Blackall. G. P. Putnam's Sons, 2010.
Gia, a young African American girl, wants to give away clothes that she has outgrown, but Mama says they should keep them. Gia knows what's coming next: "More talk about the ding-dang baby." All her friends and relatives want to talk about is the baby that Mama is having. Mama craves pecan pie, a craving that she attributes to the baby. When Mama admits

to Gia that she will miss their time alone together, Gia is comforted. Dad is never mentioned in the story, but Gia's multiracial extended family provides lots of support.

Little Rabbit's New Baby

By Harry Horse. Illustrated by the author. Peachtree, 2008.

Little Rabbit was excited to see the new baby. However, when he visits Mama in the hospital, he finds that she has had triplets. Little Rabbit is a very proud big brother and hugs, kisses, and tickles the babies. But Little Rabbit grows frustrated at what the babies can't do—eat carrots for breakfast, catch a ball, and play with his toys. He scolds the babies and decides they should leave him and his things alone. When the babies have difficulty sleeping, Little Rabbit finds that he can be a big help to his family and is a loving big brother.

Now We Have a Baby

By Lois Rock. Illustrated by Jane Massey. Good Books, 2004.

This short, sweet, and cheerful story explores life with a new baby. The book begins by pointing out some of the difficulties associated with having a new baby—for example, babies can be noisy. Then the focus shifts to the positives of having a new member in your family. Children are reminded that babies need love above all else. Love from family members will teach an infant how to smile, talk, share, and play. Large and simple print helps young readers to follow along, and pastel illustrations charmingly portray life with a new baby.

My Heart Is a Magic House

By Julie Jacobs. Illustrated by Bernadette Pons. Albert Whitman, 2007.

Stephanie, an adorable squirrel, worries that Mommy's new baby will disrupt her life. She doesn't want to share her room, but Mommy assures her that there will always be enough space. Stephanie doesn't want to share her toys, but Mommy tells her that the baby will get new toys and that her doll, Rosie, need not be shared. Realizing Stephanie's insecurity, Mommy explains that her heart grows a room for each person she loves and that the room in her heart for Stephanie will always "be just as big as it is now." Stephanie is comforted by her mother's words.

The New Baby at Your House

By Joanna Cole. Photographs by Margaret Miller. Morrow, 1998.
Cole presents straightforward information about a new baby so that older siblings will know what to expect as the baby grows. She also explores the many ways an older sibling may feel—for example, jealous, angry, prideful, and loving. The book points out the benefits of being a big kid and having more independence than the baby, aspects likely to balance feelings of jealousy. Photographs of families from different ethnic backgrounds illustrate varying situations and emotions that arise from the addition of a new baby. A lengthy note to parents provides guidance on proven techniques to aid in a child's adjustment.

What to Expect When the New Baby Comes Home

By Heidi Murkoff. Illustrated by Laura Rader. HarperFestival, 2001.
Written by a coauthor of adult favorite *What to Expect When You're Expecting*, this book provides a thorough guide to children who are about to welcome a new baby. Angus, the Answer Dog, provides responses to common questions such as "Why do new babies cry so much?" "Why can't new babies do anything by themselves?" and "Can I help take care of the new baby?" Angus also suggests games and fun thoughts that will put a positive light on the subject of new baby arrival. An introductory message to parents gives advice for easing the transition of bringing another baby into the family.

What Baby Needs

By William Sears, Martha Sears, and Christie Watts Kelly. Illustrated by Renée Andriani. Little, Brown, 2001.
Based on the concept of attachment parenting, this book explains to a child what life will be like with a new baby. The authors cover various topics—for example, why breast milk is the best food for babies, why babies like to be held close to their mommies, what causes babies to cry, and how to be a good big brother or sister. The colorful, cartoonlike illustrations present a warm and cheerful mood, and "What About Me" text boxes provide ideas for helping the older brother or sister feel important. At the beginning of the book, a page targeted toward the caregiver provides additional parenting strategies.

Another Brother

By Matthew Cordell. Illustrated by the author. Feiwel and Friends, 2012.
Davy, a single-child sheep, spends special time alone with his parents. But then Petey is born, along with eleven more brothers. Davy complains that all his brothers do is copy him—they eat the same things he eats and walk the same way he walks. Mom assures Davy that his brothers are only going through a phase, and Dad adds that they will soon have their own interests. As predicted, one day Davy finds that this is exactly the case and ends up feeling wonderfully and awfully alone. However, Davy's situation quickly changes again when a new sister arrives.

Waiting for Baby

By Harriet Ziefert. Illustrated by Emily Bolam. Henry Holt, 1998.
Max endures a long wait to become a big brother. He is curious about the baby inside his mother's tummy and asks her questions such as "How will it get out?" that are not answered in the text. Using cut pages, the book highlights ways that Max tries to get the baby out. None of his methods works, so he gives up and focuses on having fun with his parents. Finally the baby arrives, and the delighted Max holds his new sister when he visits her in the hospital.

School Days

WHAT IF I GET LOST? WHAT IF I CAN'T FIND THE *bathroom? What if my teacher is mean?* Starting school or day care is a major event in the life of a child. Some children worry more than others, of course, but almost every child feels a bit unsettled at first. The first set of books in this chapter combine humor and gentle reassurance to ease the transition for children, not to mention their parents.

Once children begin school, certain challenges may surface as tender topics from time to time. Tattling, test anxiety, cheating, learning to read, and reading motivation are addressed in the remaining selections.

Llama Llama Misses Mama

By Anna Dewdney. Illustrated by the author. Viking, 2009.
Dewdney's lovable character is about to start preschool. Little ones will feel comforted by Llama Llama's first day with his teacher and classmates, as he learns that school is fun despite missing Mama. The rhyming text

and brightly colored illustrations combine to create a story children will ask to hear again. The Llama Llama series is popular with preschool and kindergarten students.

Splat the Cat

By Rob Scotton. Illustrated by the author. HarperCollins, 2008.

Scotton's endearing character is off to his first day of Cat School. Worried about what the day will bring, he takes along Seymour, his pet mouse. As you would expect in a school full of cats, mayhem ensues. The first in a fun series of Splat the Cat books, this one is sure to strike a chord with children about to begin their own school adventures.

Maisy Goes to Preschool

By Lucy Cousins. Illustrated by the author. Candlewick, 2009.

Maisy and her friends have a lovely day at preschool. Mr. Peacock, their teacher, helps them hang their paintings in the art center, reads them a story, and makes sure they have a delicious snack. They go outside to play, and before you know it, it's time to go home. Young children already in preschool will enjoy comparing Maisy's day to their own, whereas those getting ready to start school will look forward to a day like the one Maisy experiences.

Day Care Days

By Mary Brigid Barrett. Illustrated by Patti Beling Murphy. Little, Brown, 1999.

Rhyming text describes a family's busy day. "Drop off mommy at the train. Sister goes to school again. To the day care off we go, sun or rain or sleet or snow." Comforting routines are set against a backdrop of soothing illustrations, making this a perfect selection to start or end the day, especially with young children just beginning day care.

My Preschool

By Anne Rockwell. Illustrated by the author. Henry Holt, 2008.

Preschool is Fred's favorite place to go. He excitedly takes the reader on a guided tour of his school. Young children will be charmed by his kind and welcoming teachers, fun at the water and sand tables, sharing at circle time, and, of course, storytime with a good book. Rockwell portrays a cheerful and confident child engaging with all that preschool has to offer.

Wemberly Worried

By Kevin Henkes. Illustrated by the author. Greenwillow, 2000.
Whether children are occasional or frequent worriers, they will benefit from this gentle yet powerful story. Wemberly, a shy mouse, has a tendency to worry about the crack in the living room wall, the chains on the swing in the playground, whether her friends will come to her birthday party, and even the tree in the yard. With the help of Mrs. Peachum and a special classmate, Wemberly learns to control her anxiety and have fun as she starts nursery school.

Owen

By Kevin Henkes. Illustrated by the author. Greenwillow, 1993.
When Owen's parents try explaining that he can't take his blanket to school, he doesn't want to hear it. "Fuzzy goes where I go," he exclaims. A series of humorous and unsuccessful attempts to get him to part with Fuzzy are followed by a satisfying conclusion. A classic by the prolific Henkes, *Owen* is still the perfect story to share with a young child experiencing this particular rite of passage.

Tom Goes to Kindergarten

By Margaret Wild. Illustrated by David Legge. Albert Whitman, 2000.
Tom, a young panda, is looking forward to the first day of school. He can't wait to have someone to play with, as his parents are always too busy to play with him. When his parents take him to school on the first day, however, Tom doesn't want them to leave. The teacher warmly invites the parents to stay. They have so much fun that the next day, when Tom is ready to be independent, Mommy and Daddy don't want to leave. This lively and humorous story, with cheerful watercolor illustrations, is sure to allay first-day jitters.

Kindergarten Rocks!

By Katie Davis. Illustrated by the author. Harcourt, 2005.
Dexter is just an "eensy teensy beensy bit scared" about going to kindergarten. Luckily for him, his patient big sister, Jessie, is there to reassure

him over and over that he has nothing to be afraid of because "kindergarten rocks!" Dexter soon learns that she is telling him the truth as the events of his first day unfold. Young children will see their fears addressed with love and humor in this upbeat tale.

Keisha Ann Can!

By Daniel Kirk. Illustrated by the author. G. P. Putnam's Sons, 2008.
Similar to *My Preschool* by Anne Rockwell, this story portrays a cheerful and confident child who loves school and learning. Although the grade level is not named, it appears much like kindergarten, given the activities Keisha Ann enjoys. "Who can paint a picture, and sign it with her name? Who can guess what words are missing in a rhyming game?" Questions such as these are followed by the answer "Keisha Ann can!" Kirk's bold and bright illustrations complement the spirited tone of this portrait of a motivated child enjoying a typical school day.

Countdown to Kindergarten

By Alison McGhee. Illustrated by Harry Bliss. Harcourt, 2002.
A little girl worries that she is in Big Trouble because kindergarten is starting in ten days, and she does not know how to tie her shoes. She has heard from a first grader that the number one rule in kindergarten is that you are never, ever allowed to ask for help with this. Her countdown results in the big revelation on the first day that most kids cannot tie their shoes. Bliss's detailed, comical illustrations add to the appeal of this humorous take on a common worry for many five-year-olds.

Miss Bindergarten Gets Ready for Kindergarten

By Joseph Slate. Illustrated by Ashley Wolff. Dutton, 1996.
Miss Bindergarten, a dog and the perfect kindergarten teacher, prepares to welcome her class to school on the first day. As she lovingly organizes an array of inviting learning centers, her students also prepare for the day. Using rhyming couplets, Slate introduces each of the twenty-six animals that make up the class: "Adam Krupp wakes up. Brenda Heath brushes her teeth." The charming text and engaging illustrations make this title a favorite of kindergarten students. This is one of many Miss Bindergarten selections.

How Do Dinosaurs Go to School?

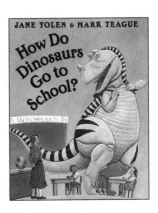

By Jane Yolen. Illustrated by Mark Teague. Blue Sky, 2007.

In a popular series for young children, Yolen and Teague's lovable dinosaur characters promote good behavior by showing the naughty counterpoint. This selection reveals the proper way to behave in school by posing questions that will delight children with their playfulness: "Does he drag his long tail? Is he late for the bus? Does he stomp all four feet? Does he make a big fuss?" This picture book is a fun choice for the first day of school.

First Day of School

By Anne Rockwell. Illustrated by Lizzy Rockwell. HarperCollins, 2011.

This story features first- or second-grade children confidently getting ready to go back to school. Friends see one another shopping for school clothes and supplies, getting new haircuts, and looking forward to the big day. Rockwell depicts school as a friendly, cheerful place where any child would want to be.

Marshall Armstrong Is New to Our School

By David Mackintosh. Illustrated by the author. Abrams, 2011.

Marshall Armstrong is different from everyone in his new school. The narrator, who sits next to him in class, describes Marshall as having freckles that look like birdseed and ears like seashells. He eats "space food" wrapped in silver wrappers, is not allowed to play sports or watch television, and has to stay in the shade outside. Unfazed by what others think of him, Marshall invites everyone to his birthday party. The narrator then describes the most amazing birthday party ever at the Armstrong home. Mackintosh's unique take on being the new kid and making friends is highly engaging.

Yoko Learns to Read

By Rosemary Wells. Illustrated by the author. Disney-Hyperion, 2012.

Yoko the kitten and her mama know their three books from Japan by heart, and they love reading them together. Yoko is proud of her three leaves on the class reading display. The problem arises when her classmates' reading skills begin to surpass her own, and Yoko has no more books she can read. After donning their best kimonos, Yoko and her mama visit the library. Book by book, Yoko begins to learn more new words, until she is really reading. This heartwarming story will reassure all children who are learning to read, whether in their primary or a secondary language. It is the latest offering in a collection by Wells featuring the adorable Yoko and her friends.

Hooray for Reading Day!

By Margery Cuyler. Illustrated by Arthur Howard. Simon and Schuster, 2008.
Jessica, a self-proclaimed worrywart, has a big worry in first grade—namely, *reading*. Reading aloud is torture. To make matters worse, her enthusiastic teacher, Mr. Martin, announces that they will have Reading Theater Day on Friday. Everyone must dress in a costume and read a line from their book in front of parents. Young children will empathize with Jessica as she practices reading to Wiggles, her dog. Practice, combined with her mom's encouragement, does the trick. The big day arrives, and Jessica triumphantly reads her part aloud. This is a reassuring title to have on hand for first graders.

I Repeat, Don't Cheat!

By Margery Cuyler. Illustrated by Arthur Howard. Simon and Schuster, 2010.
Jessica has something new to worry about. Her best friend, Lizzie, has started copying her work. Mr. Martin, the girls' teacher, has made it clear that cheating is unacceptable. Jessica decides not to tell for fear of losing her friend, but as the behavior continues, their friendship suffers. The conclusion, in which both girls face up to their mistakes and become best friends again, illustrates the natural consequences of cheating while reinforcing assertive, caring behavior.

Jamaica and the Substitute Teacher

By Juanita Havill. Illustrated by Anne Sibley O'Brien. Houghton Mifflin, 1999.
Jamaica hopes for a nice substitute while her teacher is away, and she is delighted with Mrs. Duval. The substitute teacher starts the class with a game, and when Jamaica solves the clues, she is praised in front of the class. Next they have reading groups, and Jamaica feels like singing when Mrs.

Duval praises her again. When it is time for their spelling test, Jamaica realizes she forgot to study. She copies one of the words from a classmate's paper and immediately feels guilty. Jamaica confesses to Mrs. Duval, who tells her that she doesn't have to be perfect to be special.

A Bad Case of Tattle Tongue

By Julia Cook. Illustrated by Anita DuFalla. National Center for Youth Issues, 2006.

Everyone is tired of Josh's tattling, including his classmates, his teacher, and his family. Josh's mother tells him he is going to get Tattle Tongue if he doesn't stop. Then he gets a visit from the Tattle Prince in a dream and learns all about the Tattle Rules. Cook's story offers a creative solution to a common problem in the primary grades.

Testing Miss Malarkey

By Judy Finchler. Illustrated by Kevin O'Malley. Walker, 2000.

Preparing for the upcoming I.P.T.U. (Instructional Performance Through Understanding) test has the whole school in an uproar. Miss Malarkey's students practice the Multiplication Mambo at recess and learn how to fill in the little circles properly in art class. The principal yells into the phone that he needs "the good pencils" for The Test, and the students are fed brain food in the cafeteria. This hilarious treatment of the pressures of high-stakes testing will bring a smile to everyone's face, while helping children relax before the big event.

Miss Malarkey Leaves No Reader Behind

By Judy Finchler and Kevin O'Malley. Illustrated by Kevin O'Malley. Walker, 2006.

Principal Wiggins promises to dye his hair purple and sleep on the roof of the school if his students read 1,000 books this year. The unshakable Miss Malarkey pledges to find a book for each of her students, a book each one will love reading. The narrator, who is the most reluctant reader in the class, casts an incredulous look at his classmates, who are falling under Miss Malarkey's spell and actually reading books for pleasure. The real triumph comes when he reads book 1,001, the perfect book picked by Miss Malarkey. O'Malley's comical illustrations complement this engaging story depicting the importance of reading motivation.

Physical Illness of a Child

VITALITY IS THE ENERGY OF LIFE. IT CAN BE EXPRESSED through the heart, mind, and body. Franklin Delano Roosevelt is an excellent example of someone who did not allow polio to deter him. He became one of the most energetic U.S. presidents. The author of *Treasure Island*, Robert Louis Stevenson, developed his imagination as a sick child in bed. Despite his health issues, which continued for the rest of his life, he enjoyed a prolific writing career. The books in this section help parents and children learn that good health has more to do with one's inner vitality than with being pain-free or having no illness or disease. This outlook lets children maintain their enthusiasm and involvement in life despite physical challenges.

If Beaver Had a Fever

By Helen Ketteman. Illustrated by Kevin O'Malley. Marshall Cavendish, 2011.
In this silly, upbeat, and reassuring storybook, Little Bear asks his mother, "If you were a doctor in charge of the zoo, what would you do if Gnu had

the flu?" This question starts a series of lively exchanges, with each answer colorfully drawn by Little Bear. Mama Bear would bake a cake filled with pills for Gnu's aches and chills. However, if Little Bear was sick, Mama would "puppet a story," play a tune, cuddle awhile, and blow up a balloon. The rhyming text and expressive illustrations burst with energy. O'Malley uses art markers, crayons, and colored pencils to highlight the childlike drawings of Little Bear.

Noah's Garden:
When Someone You Love Is in the Hospital

By Mo Johnson. Illustrated by Annabelle Josse. Candlewick, 2010.
Noah plays happily—flying in seaplanes, bathing with tigers, and riding on camels. "Can Jessica play in my garden?" he asks. Maybe sometime soon, his parents tell him. Noah dances with penguins, fights with pirates, and spies in helicopters. "Will Jessica ever see my garden?" Perhaps she will soon. Grandad and Noah flip a coin—plop—into the fountain, "for Jessica." One day Noah is surprised and delighted that younger sister Jessica joins him in his garden. This work was inspired by the true story of Jessica Titmus's seven-month hospital stay for a heart condition. The warm and cheerful illustrations match the family's courage and love and bring Noah's imaginative stories to life.

Iris Has a Virus

By Arlene Alda. Illustrated by Lisa Desimini. Tundra, 2008.
Although she washes her hands as Mrs. Morgan instructs, Iris does not feel quite right when she gets home from school. Iris has a stomach bug. Her brother, Doug, asks, "How are we supposed to go to Grandpa's party this Saturday?" Iris is too sick to read or draw or even watch TV. She rests, throws up, goes to the doctor, and rests some more. Friday night she dreams about all kinds of bugs—bugs that wear pants and bugs that talk! Iris wakes up refreshed. The cheerful illustrations remind us to be patient like Iris and make the best of things when we're sick with a virus.

How Do Dinosaurs Get Well Soon?

By Jane Yolen. Illustrated by Mark Teague. Blue Sky, 2003.
Many lessons can be learned from dinosaurs about what to do and what not to do when it comes to getting over the flu or a cold. Does a dinosaur

pitch his pills out the door or throw tissues on the floor or "whimper and whine"? No, of course not. He drinks plenty of juice, rests well, and willingly visits the doctor. The exuberant illustrations add to this funny and playful book with a message.

When Vera Was Sick

By Vera Rosenberry. Illustrated by the author. Henry Holt, 1998.
Vera lies in bed for many hours with chicken pox. She is too sick to color with her new crayons or do anything "except scratch her spots." Vera's family cheers her up. They put pink lotion on her spots, read a story about a little elephant, and sing to help her fall asleep. When she starts to feel a little better, Mother brings her hot soup and June plays Chinese checkers with her. Vera plays with a box of old greeting cards, making up little songs about each one. A popular children's author and illustrator, Rosenberry triumphs with this endearing story of sick Vera.

A Sick Day for Amos McGee

By Philip C. Stead. Illustrated by Erin E. Stead. Roaring Brook, 2010.
Amos McGee relishes his job at the zoo taking care of the animals. He plays chess with the elephant, races the tortoise, sits patiently with the penguin, cares for the rhinoceros, and reads storybooks to the owl. Then one day Amos wakes up with a cold and cannot go to work. The animals wait and wonder until they make their way to Amos's house. They play chess with Amos, sit quietly while he naps, hand him a handkerchief, and read him a story aloud at bedtime. The gently rendered drawings have a cheerful splash of color, perfectly matching this story about helping a friend get well.

Alfie's Attack: The Story of a Fish with Asthma

By David Bohline. Illustrated by Kelly Hopkins. Vitality, 2010.
Alfie the fish has a difficult asthma attack. He learns how to relax during the attack by using his "mind power" to imagine a calm and peaceful place. The ability to relax helps him remember where to find an inhaler. Alfie is now able to enjoy life again. Indeed, he

heroically helps his enemy the shark, who also has an asthma attack. Before D'Octopus arrives, Alfie directs the shark to imagine a calm place in the sea where you have "nothing to fear." Alfie and the shark become lifelong friends.

Going to the Hospital

By Vic Parker. Illustrated with photographs. Heinemann Library, 2011.

From Heinemann's Read and Learn series, *Going to the Hospital* uses cheerful photos and clear, uplifting text. Parker describes the logistics of a hospital and medical care; the role of doctors, nurses, and patients; reasons to go to the hospital; and more. A picture glossary and a list of dos and don'ts in the back of the book enhance the practical information in this little gem.

Do I Have to Go to the Hospital? A First Look at Going to the Hospital

By Pat Thomas. Illustrated by Lesley Harker. Barron's Educational Series, 2006.

Thomas presents a pragmatic outline for parents and children about going to the hospital. Harker's simple and warm illustrations are the perfect match to an upbeat text. Each page highlights some aspect of a hospital visit—having visitors, making friends, and listening to the doctors and nurses. Insightful questions at the bottom of the page prompt parents to encourage discussion as appropriate.

Money

NE OF THE MOST IMPORTANT LESSONS OF CHILDHOOD IS how to handle money. This learning curve starts with simple questions: Where does money come from? Why do we use money? How should we spend it? How much should we save? What does it mean to donate money? What is a budget? Books in this chapter vary from stories of impoverished families making the most of existing resources, to stories of children working hard and showing determination to achieve financial goals, to heartwarming stories of charity.

Fancy Nancy and the Fabulous Fashion Boutique

By Jane O'Connor. Illustrated by Robin Preiss Glasser. HarperCollins, 2010.
O'Connor's beloved character Fancy Nancy demonstrates generosity and money management in this fun and fancy tale. While out shopping for a birthday gift for her sister, Fancy Nancy sees a fan she wants. After purchasing her sister's gift, she doesn't have enough money for the fan. Cleverly she holds a boutique sale, selling her old dresses and accessories to

raise money. When her sister desperately wants a necklace at the sale, Fancy Nancy makes a sacrifice for her sister's happiness. Chock-full of fancy vocabulary and character-building messages, this Fancy Nancy story is a pleaser.

Little Croc's Purse

By Lizzie Finlay. Illustrated by the author. Eerdmans, 2011.

While playing, Little Croc finds a purse full of money. His friends immediately suggest spending it on lemonade and swimming. Instead Little Croc insists on honesty and brings the purse to the police. The purse's owner is grateful for its return, as it contained a special keepsake in a hidden pocket. As a reward she gives the purse and money to Little Croc, who divides the cash into spend, save, and share envelopes. He uses some of the money to bring his friends a refreshing treat. The value of honesty and money strategy are thoughtfully covered in this enjoyable story.

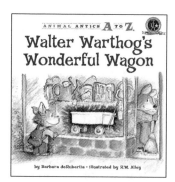

Walter Warthog's Wonderful Wagon

By Barbara deRubertis. Illustrated by R. W. Alley. Kane, 2011.

Walter Warthog sees a white wagon in the local hardware store. He wants the wagon but has no money to pay for it. The store owner suggests that Walter make deliveries for him using the wagon to earn money. Walter sets off and brings watering cans to Wendy Wombat and water skis to Wanda Weasel. In his travels the wagon gets scratched, and Wanda agrees to paint it if Walter will make a delivery for her. Walter's story teaches the value of hard work and initiative. A page providing activities for building reading skills is included.

Sweet Potato Pie

By Kathleen D. Lindsey. Illustrated by Charlotte Riley-Webb. Lee and Low, 2003.

Faced with losing their farm to the bank, Sadie's loving African American family works together to make and sell her mom's sweet potato pies at the town's Harvest Celebration. The family members split the chores—milking the cow, collecting eggs, getting flour, making butter, and preparing the sweet potatoes. The family works late into the night making the pies and is successful the next day, raising enough money to save the farm. The acrylic illustrations are colorful and flowing and add energy to the telling of the story. Mama's sweet potato pie recipe is included, providing a nice extension activity.

The Orange Shoes

By Trinka Hakes Noble. Illustrated by Doris Ettlinger. Sleeping Bear, 2007. Delly is a poor yet happy child with a loving family. Then her teacher tells the class about a Shoebox Social to raise money for art supplies. Although he can barely afford it, Delly's father buys her a new pair of shoes for the event. Delly wears them to school and is bullied by a group of mean girls, leaving her new shoes scuffed and scratched. Though heartbroken, she solves the problem by painting flowers and vines on the damaged shoes. This warm, sensitive story illustrates the power of love and of staying true to oneself.

The Berenstain Bears' Trouble with Money

Written and illustrated by Stan and Jan Berenstain. Random House, 1983. Brother and Sister Bear know a lot about Bear Country, but they do not know a lot about money. When their parents get concerned about their spendthrift ways, the cubs decide to change their behavior. They earn money selling wildflowers and berries, giving tours of Bear Country, and running a pet-minding service. Soon they have lots of money, which they try to give to their father. Papa Bear, however, does not accept the money. Instead they all go to the bank and open a savings account for the cubs. These classic characters provide a nice lesson on financial responsibility and family loyalty.

Mr. Tanen's Tie Trouble

By Maryann Cocca-Leffler. Illustrated by the author. Albert Whitman, 2003. Mr. Tanen, principal of the Lynnhurst School, loves his collection of 975 ties. Hearing there is insufficient money for the new playground that the students have been saving for, he sells his ties in a community auction to make up the deficit. Although Mr. Tanen misses his ties, he feels better when he remembers, "You have to give to get." At the playground's grand opening, Mr. Tanen is surprised to find that his ties have been returned—

linked together to form a large ribbon around the playground. The cheer-fully illustrated story brings home the idea of self-sacrifice for the greater good.

Rock, Brock, and the Savings Shock

By Sheila Bair. Illustrated by Barry Gott. Albert Whitman, 2006.
Rock and Brock are twins who are different in many ways. For doing chores, Gramps pays them each one dollar a week for ten weeks, but he adds a twist. For each dollar they save, he matches it on the next payment. Rock spends his money haphazardly, while Brock takes advantage of Gramps's deal. Consequently, Brock's earnings are substantial, while Rock saves nothing. The rhyming text and comical illustrations depict the value of savings and interest. Information at the end of the book helps children visualize how fast money can grow and provides details on interest and money-saving strategies.

The Leprechaun in the Basement

By Kathy Tucker. Illustrated by John Sandford. Albert Whitman, 1999.
Michael's disheartened dad is unemployed. His family is experiencing hard times—Michael needs new baseball shoes, and things in the home need repair. When Michael discovers O'Leary, a leprechaun, in the base-ment, he asks the elf for some gold, but O'Leary refuses. O'Leary believes that Michael is greedy, while Michael thinks O'Leary is selfish. It is left to the reader to decide if either is true. Even without giving up gold, however, O'Leary is able to help Michael and his family in other ways. In Michael's story, readers who are undergoing financial hardships will find hope that positive change is possible.

My Rows and Piles of Coins

By Tololwa M. Mollel. Illustrated by E. B. Lewis. Clarion, 1999.
In a rural Tanzanian community, Saruni longs for a bicycle to help his mother carry goods to the market. Each week he earns coins for helping her. Encouraged to spend the coins, he decides instead to save them in a special box so he can buy the bicycle. Watercolor illustrations depict the increasing amounts as Saruni periodically counts his coins in rows and piles. When he brings his savings to the bicycle salesman, the pile of coins is not enough, and Saruni is disappointed. Moved by Saruni's planning

and determination, his father gets a motorbike and sells his old bicycle to Saruni for exactly the amount he has saved.

My Very Own Room

By Amada Irma Pérez. Illustrated by Maya Christina Gonzalez. Children's Book Press, 2000.
A school-age immigrant Mexican girl with five younger brothers dreams of having her own room. With little space in her family's house, she asks that a small storage area be cleared out and turned into her room. Using left-over paint, a hand-me-down bed, a makeshift night table, and a stack of library books to furnish her space, she feels like the happiest, luckiest girl in the world. The complete text is provided in both Spanish and English. The family's resourcefulness and supporting nature provide a positive portrayal of families living under difficult financial circumstances.

My Heart Will Not Sit Down

By Mara Rockliff. Illustrated by Ann Tanksley. Knopf, 2012.
Inspired by events during the Great Depression, a girl in Cameroon, Africa, becomes committed to raising money to help starving children in her teacher's village of New York City. Kedi feels a great deal of sympathy for these hungry American children and asks people in her village to donate. Her only success is a small coin her mother gives her, but later the villagers come forward to contribute as well. Speaking for the group, the headman says, "Our hearts would not sit down until we helped." A comprehensive author's note explains the details of the true story.

Beatrice's Goat

By Page McBrier. Illustrated by Lori Lohstoeter. Atheneum, 2001.
Beatrice and her five siblings live with their mother in Uganda. They consider themselves lucky when they receive a goat as a gift from people far away. Their new goat soon gives birth to twins, and Beatrice finds she enjoys caring for the three animals. By selling goat milk at the market, Beatrice saves enough money to go to school. Lus-

cious, large illustrations of African plants and daily life fill the pages and make this story based on true events a visual treat. An afterword by Hillary Rodham Clinton describes the work of Heifer International.

One Hen: How One Small Loan Made a Big Difference

By Katie Smith Milway. Illustrated by Eugenie Fernandes. Kids Can, 2008. Kojo lives with his mother in a small village in Ghana. The families who live in the village have little money, so they pool their savings to loan to one family to purchase something important. When it is Kojo's mother's turn, Kojo asks her if he can buy a hen so that they can have eggs to eat and sell. She agrees, and soon he has saved enough to expand his business and return to school. Eventually he has enough money to help many people in his community. Sunny, African-themed illustrations enhance the tale, and the final pages tell the true story that inspired this work.

Moving

CHILDREN FACE MANY UNKNOWNS WHEN THEIR FAMILY MOVES. The change can produce great excitement or trigger apprehension and anxiety. Children may feel sad to be leaving old friends behind, or they may be nervous about getting established in a new neighborhood or school. Children should be reassured that they can take their things with them, that they will make new friends, and that they will be able to keep in touch and continue relationships with their old friends. Stories can help children discover that moving is a way to expand their horizons and open up new opportunities. They become confident that in time they will become comfortable in their new home and environment. Books also explain the process of moving, which can take many of the scary unknowns out of the situation.

Big Ernie's New Home:
A Story for Children Who Are Moving

Written and illustrated by Teresa and Whitney Martin. Magination, 2006.
Big Ernie the cat loves his San Francisco home and his daily walking adventures with Little Henry. When Little Henry is unable to take Big Ernie on his walk because it is time to pack for their family's move, Big Ernie becomes very worried. In time, comforted by familiar tuna breakfasts and favorite chair snuggles, Big Ernie ventures out to look around his new Santa Fe home. Eventually he accepts the move and regains his confidence to seek new adventures with Little Henry. End pages offer suggestions for "explaining the move," "timing the news," and "reducing stress" for children.

Boomer's Big Day

By Constance W. McGeorge. Illustrated by Mary Whyte. Chronicle, 1994.
Told through the eyes of an adorable golden retriever named Boomer, this story chronicles a family's move. Boomer first discovers it's not an ordinary day as the family bustles about and strange boxes appear. Poor Boomer does not understand what is going on, but he does realize that a lot of strange things are happening. Once the family is unpacked at their new home, Boomer finds his missing toys and even makes new friends. Preschool children facing a move will find much similarity between their own feelings and situations and those of Boomer.

Half a World Away

By Libby Gleeson. Illustrated by Freya Blackwood. Arthur A. Levine, 2007.
Louie's best friend, Amy, has moved to the other side of the world. It used to be when either friend called "Coo-ee," the other would be there in a flash. Now parted, the friends miss each other immensely. Louie uses his loudest voice to send his "Coo-ee, Am-ee" call through the clouds and across the ocean. That night Amy dreams Louie is calling her. Through unique use of color, superb watercolor illustrations skillfully represent the children's moods. Amy and Louie's story demonstrates that regardless of distance, a special connection can be maintained.

Moving

By Vic Parker. Illustrated with photographs. Heinemann Library, 2011.
In this nonfiction book, simple text describes the process of moving, and vocabulary words such as *apartment* and *neighborhood* are introduced in boldface. Photographs of ethnically diverse families show them preparing to move, engaging in activities such as sorting items to donate or keep, packing boxes, and cleaning their old homes. The book shows moving day and offers advice for staying in touch with old friends and meeting new friends and neighbors. A small picture glossary and a detailed table of contents are included.

I Like Where I Am

By Jessica Harper. Illustrated by G. Brian Karas. G. P. Putnam's Sons, 2004.
Using rhyming text and comical illustrations, this book tells of a six-year-old boy who loves his house on Willow Street. He likes his school, enjoys living close to a swimming pool, and has a best friend who lives down the block. But the boy has big trouble because the moving men have come to take his family and his things to Little Rock, Arkansas, which is far away. The sad boy cries on his mother's lap. After the move he is just as happy in his new home yet maintains sweet memories of his home on Willow Street.

The Berenstain Bears' Moving Day

Written and illustrated by Stan and Jan Berenstain. Random House, 1981.
The Berenstain Bear family didn't always live in a tree house; there was a time that they lived happily in a comfortable and cozy hillside cave. When trees for Papa's work become scarce and the difficulty of raising vegetables becomes tiresome, they decide to move into the valley. When Mama and Papa Bear explain the moving process to Brother Bear, he is apprehensive at first, but then he becomes excited about moving to their new home. Many children know and love the Berenstain Bears and will enjoy discovering how they moved into their famed tree house.

We Are Best Friends

By Aliki. Illustrated by the author. Greenwillow, 1982.
It is tough when you are left behind when your best friend moves away. When Peter tells Robert that he is moving, Robert insists that Peter stay. Robert becomes very sad and lonely after Peter moves. The two exchange

letters, and when Robert learns that Peter has made a new friend, he ventures befriending a new boy at school. The illustrations of the boys in action are inviting and expressive of their varied emotions. Peter and Robert's story will be reassuring to children who are facing separation from a special friend.

Homegrown House

By Janet S. Wong. Illustrated by E. B. Lewis. Margaret K. McElderry, 2009. An eight-year-old girl contemplates her family's move to their fourth house. At first she does not want to move, dislikes house hunting, and cannot imagine a better home than the one she already has. After talking with her understanding and sensitive grandmother, she realizes that in time she can again settle into a new house, love it, and set it up just right to make it truly home. Gorgeous watercolor illustrations enhance the soft, comforting feel of the story as the girl progresses from feeling pessimistic about moving to looking forward to planning for her new home.

14

Military Families

WITH THE RISE IN MILITARY DEPLOYMENT OVER-seas, many families now face lengthy separations. Such parting can lead to stress and uncertainty for children. It can also present opportunities for children to understand and honor the role their parent or loved one is playing in helping to protect the nation. Sharing a picture book about characters in similar circumstances can be comforting for the entire family. Books that depict military families dealing with separation together help children cope with this unusual burden. The picture books in this chapter are uplifting and patriotic, depicting both moms and dads who treasure their families as well as their service to this country. Some stories end with a joyous homecoming, while others portray the family awaiting a loved one's return.

While You Are Away

By Eileen Spinelli. Illustrated by Renée Graef. Hyperion, 2004.

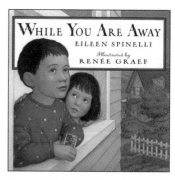

"While you are on that big ship, Daddy, far, far away, I wonder about you." Spinelli has captured the essence of how children feel as they wait for their parents to return. In three simple vignettes, a boy misses his father who is away at sea, a girl misses her mother who is serving as a pilot, and another boy misses his father who is driving a jeep. Graef's illustrations are a perfect match for the comforting prose. The two-page spread depicting the families' joyful reunions provides an uplifting conclusion to the three tales.

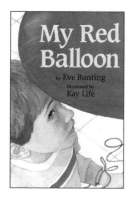

My Red Balloon

By Eve Bunting. Illustrated by Kay Life. Boyds Mills, 2005.

The big day has finally arrived: Daddy is returning home after being away at sea. Bobby is excited to go with his mom to greet his father at the dock. A red heart-shaped balloon with the words *Welcome Home* gets away from him as the ship pulls into the harbor, and Bobby is afraid his father won't know him in the crowd. Never fear—his dad spots him right away. This heartwarming story and the joyful reunion depicted in Life's illustrations will help families prepare for a military homecoming.

Sometimes We Were Brave

By Pat Brisson. Illustrated by France Brassard. Boyds Mills, 2010.

In this personal narrative told from a child's perspective, Jerome shares the story of how he, his dad, and his dog, Duffy, cope with Mom's being away at sea. Warm and sensitive, this story is realistic in its depiction of good days and bad days. Dad takes good care of them, and mishaps are handled in a calm, loving manner. Although the story does not end in the usual joyful homecoming, it is very hopeful, as Jerome looks forward to Mom returning and discovering that he has been brave in her absence. This book is a good choice for children with a parent in active service.

When Dad's at Sea

By Mindy L. Pelton. Illustrated by Robert G. Steele. Albert Whitman, 2004.
Emily's dad, a navy pilot, is soon leaving for a six-month tour of duty on an aircraft carrier. Mom and Dad construct a paper chain to help Emily count the days until his return. Each day she is cheered by the notes and pictures her father has hidden in the links. She looks forward to the day the chain will be gone and he will be home again. The passage of time is handled in a comforting yet realistic way, and the conclusion is satisfying as Dad returns home to his loving family. Steele's watercolor illustrations complement the gentle tone of the story.

Stars Above Us

By Geoffrey Norman. Illustrated by E. B. Lewis. G. P. Putnam's Sons, 2009.
Amanda's father helps her overcome her fear of the dark by showing her the wonders of the night sky. Knowing he will be shipped overseas soon, he decorates her bedroom ceiling with glow-in-the-dark stars. He tells her the North Star will be their special connection while he is away and gives her a puppy named Bear, for the Big Dipper. A hopeful look at separation in which the father returns home at the end, this book will provide comfort while helping children understand that periods of separation are often an unavoidable part of life.

The Impossible Patriotism Project

By Linda Skeers. Illustrated by Ard Hoyt. Dial, 2007.
Caleb's teacher assigns a challenging project for honoring Presidents' Day. Each student must make something that depicts patriotism for a Parents' Night celebration. His classmates spring into action: Hannah decides to craft a model of the Liberty Bell, Kareem plans to draw a colorful map of the fifty states, and Molly chooses to dress up as the Statue of Liberty. But Caleb doesn't know where to begin. Finally, he thinks of the perfect project: a picture of his dad, who is serving in the military overseas. The heartwarming conclusion celebrates the essence of patriotism.

Night Catch

By Brenda Ehrmantraut. Illustrated by Vicki Wehrman. Bubble Gum, 2005.
Facing deployment halfway around the world, a father finds a way to stay connected to his young son by playing a nightly game of catch with

the North Star. This sweet story told in rhyming verse appeals to all age groups. "Back and forth our star will fly, racing through the nighttime sky." Though very young children may not grasp the concept, they will enjoy the lyrical text and Wehrman's cheerful, soothing illustrations.

The Invisible String

By Patrice Karst. Illustrated by Geoff Stevenson. DeVorss, 2000.
Frightened by a storm, Liza and Jeremy awake and want to stay close to their mother. She comforts them by explaining that they are always together, connected by an invisible string made of love. As the children pose faraway situations and places where the string couldn't possibly reach, the mother reassures them over and over that it reaches anywhere and everywhere. A comforting picture book for families facing separation, *The Invisible String*'s cheerful illustrations and timeless message of the power of love will inspire children and adults.

Love, Lizzie: Letters to a Military Mom

By Lisa Tucker McElroy. Illustrated by Diane Paterson. Albert Whitman, 2005.
A collection of letters and drawings between a daughter and her mom who is serving overseas, this unique picture book is a great choice for older children. In her frequent letters, Lizzie tells her mom about her soccer games, the new ice cream store down the street, and other daily events. She includes detailed maps so her mother can picture the places she is describing. Paterson's brightly colored illustrations create a cheerful tone. The book includes a list of tips for parents on how to help their children handle separation.

Pilot Mom

By Kathleen Benner Duble. Illustrated by Alan Marks. Charlesbridge, 2003.
Jenny and her best friend, K.C., spend the day with Jenny's mom, an air force tanker pilot. Jenny is proud to show K.C. around the base, but she is worried about her mother's upcoming training mission. As they interact throughout the tour, it becomes clear that mother and daughter have a close, loving relationship. Jenny is comforted by the fact that her mother is calm and competent under pressure, though she worries about her when she flies. Duble provides a model of a strong woman who loves both her family and her job, serving her country with pride.

Red, White, and Blue Good-bye

By Sarah Wones Tomp. Illustrated by Ann Barrow. Walker, 2005.
"Daddy is a navy man, a sailor man, a brave man." A little girl is having a difficult time telling her daddy good-bye as he prepares to leave on a six-month voyage. Daddy remains loving and patient as she climbs into his sea bag to go with him and hides his big black boots so he can't leave. He comforts her with reassuring family rituals like Magnificent 'Mazing Milkshakes, and cheers her up with a special red, white, and blue good-bye. Red flags, white clouds, blue ocean—the softly hued images provide a soothing backdrop for young children learning to say good-bye.

My Big Brother

By Miriam Cohen. Illustrated by Ronald Himler. Star Bright, 2005.
In this story of brotherly love, a young boy (the middle child in the family) tells the reader about his big brother, whom he clearly idolizes. His much older brother teaches him many important things—how to shoot baskets, wash a car, and talk nicely to his mother. When his big brother goes into the army, the boy tries to fill the void by being a good big brother to their youngest sibling, but he dearly misses his older brother. This is a touching and honest portrayal of a family carrying on while waiting for a loved one to return.

H Is for Honor: A Military Family Alphabet

By Devin Scillian. Illustrated by Victor Juhasz. Sleeping Bear, 2006.
In this innovative alphabet book, Scillian, the son of a career army officer, combines a rhyming text for each letter with a sidebar of information on the topic. Juhasz's detailed illustrations complement the respectful tone of the text. "Not everyone hears it. It's just a few. But there's no denying it once you do. When your country calls, you do your part. So H is for honor in the American heart." On the accompanying page is found the military oath of allegiance and information on Crispus Attucks, the first American to give his life in the American Revolution. Going beyond a simple ABC book, *H Is for Honor* is an engaging primer on all things military.

My Dad's a Hero

By Rebecca Christiansen and Jewel Armstrong. Illustrated by Jen O. Robertson. Word Association Publishers, 2007.
A slim paperback with a powerful message and an uplifting tone, *My*

Dad's a Hero will help young children understand the concept of military sacrifice. Most important, the book addresses many questions children may have about their parent's service in a way that will leave them feeling proud to have a military dad.

Hero Dad

By Melinda Hardin. Illustrated by Bryan Langdo. Marshall Cavendish, 2010.

"My dad is a superhero." A little boy compares a comic superhero to his dad, a real-life superhero serving in the army. Instead of rocket-propelled boots, Dad wears army boots. Instead of a cloak that makes him invisible, he wears camouflage. Hardin's simple text and Langdo's illustrations of army life combine to give age-appropriate information to young children on what makes a soldier a real hero.

Adoption

NTERTAINING PICTURE BOOKS ARE AN EXCELLENT WAY TO introduce *all* children to the concept of adoption. These books can give adoptees the confidence to voice their own fears and questions—and help all children view adoption as a natural, loving part of life. A discussion about adoption can be initiated by reading a good picture book.

Many of the books selected for this chapter focus on specific dimensions of adoption: international adoption, interracial adoption, single-parent adoption, same-sex-partner adoption, open adoption, older child adoption, and the needs of siblings anticipating their newly adopted brother or sister.

A Mother for Choco

By Keiko Kasza. Illustrated by the author. G. P. Putnam's Sons, 1992.
Choco is an adorable little bird who wishes he had a mother. Thinking his mother will look like him, he asks animals with similar traits if they are his mother. All answer in the negative, citing a physical difference. This makes Choco so sad that he cries, which sends Mrs. Bear running to see what the

trouble is. She playfully assures him that physical differences don't matter in motherhood and asks to be his mother. This sweetly illustrated story shows that it is love and caring that are important in a family, not what the family members look like.

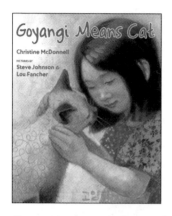

Goyangi Means Cat

By Christine McDonnell. Illustrated by Steve Johnson and Lou Fancher. Viking, 2011.
This international story expresses how difficult it can be for a young child to adjust to a new family in a foreign place. Soo Min comes to live with her adopted white American family. She does not speak English, and her parents know only a few Korean words. Most things are strange to her, but she loves the family cat, Goyangi, right away. When Goyangi goes missing and then reappears, Soo Min realizes that she has "found her true home too." Korean characters are creatively incorporated into the luscious illustrations, and transliterated Korean words are used in the story.

Jin Woo

By Eve Bunting. Illustrated by Chris K. Soentpiet. Clarion, 2001.
David's parents are ecstatically anticipating the arrival of their adopted baby, Jin Woo, who is from Korea. They have painted Jin Woo's room and set up his crib. David, on the other hand, is uncertain about getting a new brother. He wonders if his parents were as excited when they adopted him and if they will still love him as much. When the baby arrives, reassurance from his parents and a first smile from Jin Woo change David's feelings, and his love for Jin Woo quickly grows. Striking, eye-catching watercolor illustrations effectively convey the deep emotions of the family members.

Sweet Moon Baby: An Adoption Tale

By Karen Henry Clark. Illustrated by Patrice Barton. Knopf, 2010.
A perfect baby girl is born in China one summer night. Her parents are too poor to care for her and to provide the things they want for her. They trust the moon and put the baby in a basket on the river to float to her future. On the other side of the world, her adoptive parents prepare and wait for her until one night the moon signals them to find their sweet moon baby.

This imaginative book focuses on international adoption and is a good choice for fans of fairy tales and those who believe in destiny.

We Belong Together: A Book about Adoption and Families
By Todd Parr. Illustrated by the author. Little, Brown, 2007.
Parr cheerfully captures what it means for a family to belong together. With bright and boldly colorful pictures, he illustrates the love a family feels for its adoptive child. This book is flexible enough to be appropriate for any family structure. All kinds of families, including interracial and same-sex parents, are represented in the artful drawings. The focus is on the adoptive child's needs, such as to be read to or to be loved, and the adoptive parents' ability to fulfill those needs. The text is simple and clear, making this a good choice for young children.

I Love You Like Crazy Cakes
By Rose Lewis. Illustrated by Jane Dyer. Little, Brown, 2000.
Lewis tells the loving story of how she adopted her Chinese baby girl. Wanting to adopt, a woman flies to China and meets the baby she has dreamt of for years. At the end of the baby's first day in America, the woman rocks her new daughter to sleep and hopes that her Chinese mother knows that the baby is safe and happy. This delightful story, illustrated with watercolor portrayals of mother and baby, introduces the concept of international adoption.

Tell Me Again about the Night I Was Born
By Jamie Lee Curtis. Illustrated by Laura Cornell. HarperCollins, 1996.
This story stands out because the narrator is the adopted child. The child begs to hear the story of the night she was born—how her parents rushed to the hospital to meet her and what happened on her first night at home. The child knows this story well, as she must have been told it many times. Clearly the retellings make her feel much loved and extraordinarily special. The comical, cartoon-style illustrations add humor and fun to this happy story that affirms bountiful parental love.

We Are Adopted
By Jennifer Moore-Mallinos. Illustrated by Rosa M. Curto. Barron's Educational Series, 2007.
This nonfiction book is narrated by the older sibling of a newly adopted baby. Both children have been adopted from different cities in Russia. The

family is thrilled to introduce their new child to everyday American life, while also educating both children about their cultural heritage. Suggestions for craft projects that honor a child's birth country are appealing. The book offers guidelines for parents about their own physical and emotional concerns and offers suggestions for talking to a child about adoption.

Mommy Far, Mommy Near: An Adoption Story

By Carol Antoinette Peacock. Illustrated by Shawn Costello Brownell. Albert Whitman, 2000.

This longer story about a Chinese girl who questions her circumstance is both touching and hugely sentimental. Warmly colored illustrations capture the emotions of each character. Through healthy games of pretend, Elizabeth comes to terms with having a birth mother who lives far away and an adoptive mother who lives with her. Her adoptive mother gives comfort by reminding Elizabeth that she is her child and will be loved by the family forever. This reassuring story addresses some of the emotional complications that can arise with international adoption.

I'm Adopted!

By Shelley Rotner and Sheila M. Kelly. Photographs by Shelley Rotner. Holiday House, 2011.

Simple and clear text touches on some key concepts of and questions about adoption, including reasons why birth mothers may not keep their children. The text and expressive, colorful photographs communicate that children will feel happy in their adoptive families when they are cared for and loved. The photographs also depict children from varying ethnic backgrounds who have been adopted by all kinds of families, including gay couples and single parents. The book describes how adopted children often like to learn about and visit their birth country and how they want to hear their particular adoption story "again and again."

I Wished for You: An Adoption Story

By Marianne Richmond. Illustrated by the author. Sourcebooks, 2010.

Nothing can beat the feeling of being someone's wish come true. In this heartwarming story, Mama Bear tells her son, Barley Bear, about how he is her wish come true. She explains she had an empty place she wanted to fill with love and says, "Of all the children in the whole wide world, God picked *you* for me." This story is fitting for a single mother, for a child who was adopted at an older age, and for interracial adoption. It stresses that what is really important is that members of a family love each other.

Happy Adoption Day!

By John McCutcheon. Illustrated by Julie Paschkis. Little, Brown, 1996.
"Some parents come different, some come the same, / But whether they're single or pairs, / You're never alone, you're always at home / Whenever there's love we can share." These are the lyrics of the song "Happy Adoption Day," which is the foundation of this book. The words are enhanced by bright, joyful, folksy illustrations that recognize many types of families. Simple musical notation is included. A white couple reminisces about when they prepared for and traveled home with their newly adopted Asian baby. The song celebrates the anniversary of this adoption. Its fun rhyme scheme makes it particularly great for read-alouds.

Learning Disabilities and Behavior Issues

CHILDREN WITH SPECIAL NEEDS, SUCH AS THOSE WHO HAVE Asperger syndrome, autism, dyslexia, or attention deficit hyperactivity disorder (ADHD), have an extra hurdle to overcome in school and in life. It is important for children to recognize that these hurdles are unique challenges, not obstacles in their path to learning and personal growth. Understanding is key to a child's positive self-concept and acceptance by others. The books chosen for this chapter help children and adults alike recognize the many talents and gifts one can possess, regardless of a learning challenge.

Thank You, Mr. Falker

By Patricia Polacco. Illustrated by the author. Philomel, 1998.
Polacco shares her personal struggle with dyslexia in this moving story based on her own childhood. Young Trisha loves books and is eager to start school and learn to read. Sadly, that promise is not fulfilled, as each year

she struggles and falls further behind. The cruel taunts of her classmates cause her to withdraw and attempt to hide her disability. Then she finds herself in fifth grade with a new teacher, Mr. Falker. He recognizes her artistic ability, uncovers the secret she has been hiding, and gets Trisha the help she needs. The heartwarming resolution will leave children hopeful and adults inspired.

The Junkyard Wonders

By Patricia Polacco. Illustrated by the author. Philomel, 2010.
Another book based on true events from Polacco's childhood, this inspirational story tells of the year Trisha spends in a new school in Michigan. Trisha is deeply disappointed to learn she has been placed in Room 206, a special class. The classroom is named "the junkyard" by other students, because all the kids in it learn differently. Trisha soon discovers that her amazing teacher, Mrs. Peterson, doesn't allow any of her students to feel like an outcast. Instead, she encourages them to embrace their unique gifts and explore their potential. This book is best shared with older children (grades three through five).

The Alphabet War: A Story about Dyslexia

By Diane Burton Robb. Illustrated by Gail Piazza. Albert Whitman, 2004.
Adam loves being read to in his preschool years and starts kindergarten knowing many familiar stories. But when he is faced with the task of learning about letters and sounds, nothing seems to stick. His active imagination soon begins to wage "the alphabet war" with letters and words. After Adam is diagnosed with dyslexia, a reading specialist begins the slow process of teaching him to read and building his confidence. This insightful story presents a realistic yet uplifting look at the challenges of dyslexia.

My Friend Has Autism

By Amanda Doering Tourville. Illustrated by Kristin Sorra. Picture Window, 2010.
This book is part of the Friends with Disabilities series. In this story, Nick tells the reader about his friend Zack, who has autism. Zack knows more

about airplanes than anyone Nick knows, and they enjoy building model planes together. Nick understands that he has to bring his own models to Zack's house, because Zack doesn't like anyone touching his things.

The Friends with Disabilities books are simply told stories with fact boxes inserted throughout and back matter offering additional information about the disability. The books in this series include *My Friend Has Dyslexia*, *My Friend Has ADHD*, and *My Friend Has Down Syndrome*. Their underlying message of acceptance and friendship makes them excellent choices for helping children and adults understand the characteristics of these learning disabilities.

Ian's Walk: A Story about Autism

By Laurie Lears. Illustrated by Karen Ritz. Albert Whitman, 1998.
Julie takes her younger, autistic brother, Ian, for a walk in the park and experiences a range of emotions along the way. This is a sensitive, realistic story of two siblings and the complex relationship they share. During the walk together, Julie experiences confusion, annoyance, embarrassment, love, and appreciation for Ian and his different way of experiencing the world. The facial expressions portrayed in the illustrations add to the array of emotions conveyed in this simple, sweet story. The book includes front matter by a child psychologist on siblings of children with autism.

All Cats Have Asperger Syndrome

By Kathy Hoopmann. Illustrated with photographs. Jessica Kingsley, 2006.
The charming photographs and touching, humorous descriptions make a wonderful introduction to what it means to be a person with Asperger syndrome. This book was recognized by the Children's Book Council of Australia. Another equally engaging title by Hoopmann, *All Dogs Have ADHD*, is also available through Jessica Kingsley Publishers.

Mrs. Gorski, I Think I Have the Wiggle Fidgets

By Barbara Esham. Illustrated by Mike and Carl Gordon. Mainstream Connections, 2008.
David Sheldon is constantly doing things that upset his teacher, Mrs. Gorski—much to his dismay, as he never seems to realize it until after the fact. David overhears his father talking about how he had "the wiggle fidgets" as a child and comes up with his own creative and practical plan to

help himself behave. This book is an excellent resource for understanding ADHD and is part of an innovative series. Barbara Esham's Adventures of Everyday Geniuses books received the 2008 Parents' Choice Award, were featured on American Library Association book lists, and have been recommended by Reading Rockets. Titles include *Last to Finish: A Story about the Smartest Boy in Math Class*; *If You're So Smart, How Come You Can't Spell Mississippi?*; and *Stacey Coolidge's Fancy-Smancy Cursive Handwriting*.

Ms. McCaw Learns to Draw

By Kaethe Zemach. Illustrated by the author. Arthur A. Levine, 2008.
Dudley Ellington struggles with learning new concepts and isn't "very good at paying attention" in class. His teacher, Ms. McCaw, encourages him every step of the way and makes learning fun for her students. They believe she can do anything, until one day she attempts to draw a person's profile on the board and admits she can't do it. Dudley demonstrates and encourages Ms. McCaw until she is successful. She then cancels math and devotes the rest of the day to art. This cheerful, heartwarming story illustrates that there are many different types of talents.

17

Diversity

ART OF THE JOY OF DISCOVERY IN THE LIVES OF YOUNG children lies in learning that not everyone is identical to them. The world is filled with different religions, cultures, languages, skin colors, family customs, and traditions. Books can be windows that allow us to see, appreciate, and explore this world and learn about individual people. They can also help us recognize, appreciate, and learn about our commonality. Children in minority situations can find images and stories of children like themselves, which can foster self-esteem.

Ten Little Fingers and Ten Little Toes

By Mem Fox. Illustrated by Helen Oxenbury. Harcourt, 2008.

Fantastic for storytimes aimed at even the youngest audience, this rhyming story is charmingly illustrated with big images of babies from around the world. The singsong text and the refrain—"And both of these babies, as everyone knows, had ten little fingers and ten little toes"—are extremely catchy and will soon have listeners joining in. The babies, introduced in pairs, are born in different circumstances (in town, in the hills, on the ice, or in a tent), but they all have the most basic attribute in common: ten little fingers and ten little toes.

It's Okay to Be Different

By Todd Parr. Illustrated by the author. Little, Brown, 2001.
The bright colors and thick lines of Parr's characteristic style celebrate the things that make us all unique. However we look and whatever we like to do, it's okay and it's acceptable. Whether we have big ears, wear glasses, were adopted, are a different color, or come from somewhere else—it's all okay. It's also okay to "make a wish," "talk about your feelings," and "do something nice for yourself." Parr's light, humorous style makes this a very accessible book for introducing children to the concepts of tolerance, self-acceptance, mutual respect, and diversity.

One World, One Day

By Barbara Kerley. Illustrated with photographs. National Geographic Society, 2009.
Exquisite photography and brief text illuminate a day in the lives of children all over the world. As dawn breaks, children everywhere rise, wash, and eat breakfast. Whether breakfast consists of toast or churros, regardless of where children live and what culture they belong to, the basics of their daily lives—waking up, eating meals, going to school, spending time with their families, and getting ready for bed—are the same. The book includes an author's note about the spirit behind the work as well as detailed information about each photograph.

Bread, Bread, Bread

By Ann Morris. Photographs by Ken Heyman. Lothrop, Lee and Shepard, 1989.
People all over the world make and eat bread. Bread comes in all shapes and sizes—it can be long or short, flat or thick, and even made into pizza or pretzels. Eating bread will help you grow and be strong. Photographs of people making, eating, and selling all types of bread illustrate that it is something we all have in common. The text is minimal, allowing the pho-

tos to convey the message. An index provides the country of origin and a brief explanation for twenty-five of the photos.

Shades of People

By Shelley Rotner and Sheila M. Kelly. Photographs by Shelley Rotner. Holiday House, 2009.

"Have you noticed that people come in many different shades? Not colors, exactly, but shades." So begins this engaging exploration into the beautiful variety of skin color. Whether skin is almond, coffee, pink, peach, copper, or brown, you can't tell what a person is like based on her color because "our skin is just our covering, like wrapping paper." Exceptional, interesting photographs show people of all ages and ethnicities engaged in fun activities. The text is very brief but effectively conveys the point. This book makes a perfect introduction to the topic and is well suited for preschoolers.

The Colors of Us

By Karen Katz. Illustrated by the author. Henry Holt, 1999.

Lena is the color of cinnamon. Her artist mom teaches her that there are many shades of brown skin. While walking through their community, they notice the many different colors of people, comparing each to a food or a color found in nature. Katz uses brightly colored collage, gouache, and pencil to bring to life the people Lena and her mom encounter. This positive, lively story celebrates the many shades of brown skin.

Whoever You Are

By Mem Fox. Illustrated by Leslie Staub. Harcourt Brace, 1997.

This Reading Rainbow book begins by observing differences among children around the world—differences in the types of houses they live in, differences in the color of their skin, and differences in the words they use. Then the focus shifts to the similarities among the children—"their hearts are just like yours," and their smiles, laughs, and hurts are, too. Each illustration is presented in a carved, jeweled picture frame, extending the theme that both our differences and our similarities are to be recognized and celebrated.

Black, White, Just Right!

By Marguerite W. Davol. Illustrated by Irene Trivas. Albert Whitman, 1993.
A girl with a black mother and a white father describes the many ways that being somewhat like each of them makes her just right. Her mama's hair is black and somewhat curly, while her papa's hair is popcorn-colored and straight. The girl's hair is in between and just right. Mama is short, while Papa is six feet tall. The girl knows that her height will be just right. The book compares the parents' physical attributes and their personal tastes to emphasize that skin color is just another characteristic that makes each person unique.

All the Colors of the Earth

By Sheila Hamanaka. Illustrated by the author. Morrow, 1994.
Colorful paintings that span two pages and poetic text liken the various tones of children's skin and hair to natural things in the world—"roaring browns of bears," "whispering golds of late summer grasses," and "hair like bouncing baby lambs." The book illustrates that love comes in many colors by depicting multiracial families in loving and happy situations. Children holding hands, jumping for joy, and putting their arms around each other make this book a beautiful celebration of ethnic diversity.

Children around the World

By Donata Montanari. Illustrated by the author. Kids Can, 2001.
The world is filled with children who have many different hair colors, skin colors, and clothing. Meet children from twelve different countries and learn a bit about what life is like for each of them. Whether it is Emilio from the Philippines, Malaika from Tanzania, or Stavros from Greece, you will find similarities and differences among them all. Cheerful, paper collage illustrations help children visualize unique items from each child's homeland. An engaging introduction to the wonderful diversity among people around the world, this resource may motivate children to learn more about their counterparts in other countries.

My Nose, Your Nose

By Melanie Walsh. Illustrated by the author. Houghton Mifflin, 2002.
Using few words and large, brightly colored illustrations, this book provides a reminder that although people have physical differences, they share many common traits. For example, Daisy and Agnes have different

skin colors, but they both have pink tongues. Agnes, Kit, Arthur, and Daisy have different eye colors, but they all close their eyes when they try to go to sleep. The large print and simple shapes make this book ideal for toddlers.

Shades of Black: A Celebration of Our Children

By Sandra L. Pinkney. Photographs by Myles C. Pinkney. Scholastic, 2000.
A feeling of pride is expressed in the phrase "I am Black, I am Unique," and it is repeated several times, heightening this celebration of the beautiful variety of physical features of black children. Pinkney describes the many shades of black skin represented in the photographs of children. The text explores the range of black skin color from creamy white like vanilla ice cream to midnight blue like a licorice stick. Black hair textures and styles as well as gemlike eye colors are noted and appreciated. This book creatively explores diversity within a racial group.

The Sandwich Swap

By Her Majesty Queen Rania Al Abdullah with Kelly DiPucchio. Illustrated by Tricia Tusa. Disney-Hyperion, 2010.
Lily and Salma do a lot of things together because they are best friends. Every day at school they eat lunch together; Lily always eats a peanut butter and jelly sandwich, and Salma always eats a hummus and pita sandwich. Silently, each thinks the other's sandwich is strange and gross. When their thoughts are spoken, the girls argue. Classmates overhear, and soon everyone is name-calling. The story ends happily when the students have an international picnic and come to appreciate their differences. Inspired by the Queen of Jordan's own childhood, this child-friendly story teaches cross-cultural tolerance and acceptance.

18

Vision, Hearing, and Mobility Issues

FOCUSING ON ABILITIES RATHER THAN DISABILITIES, THE books in this chapter support understanding of children with disabilities. By using senses that are not impaired, kids with disabilities lead lives that are as full as those of their able-bodied peers. Just like other children, they go to school, have friends, play sports, take care of pets, act in plays, and have a range of feelings. Whether blind, deaf, or possessing mobility issues, children can adapt to their circumstances brilliantly and lead productive lives. They have loving relationships with their families and healthy friendships with their peers.

Through Grandpa's Eyes

By Patricia MacLachlan. Illustrated by Deborah Ray. Harper and Row, 1980.
In this Reading Rainbow book, John likes Grandpa's house best of all because he can see everything as his blind Grandpa does—by using senses other than sight. Together they smell eggs and toast for breakfast, hear the

birds sing, and feel the sun and the wind as Grandpa teaches John how to see and appreciate the world without vision. The close, loving relationship between John and his active grandfather helps children understand how blind people can lead happy, fulfilling lives by compensating with their other senses.

The Black Book of Colors

By Menena Cottin. Illustrated by Rosana Faría. Translated by Elisa Amado. Groundwood, 2008.

Children experience this book by feeling the illustrations, which are raised, black-line drawings on a solid black background. The text, provided in white font and braille, describes how Thomas experiences colors using touch, taste, smell, and sound. "Red is sour like unripe strawberries," and "It hurts when he finds it on his scraped knee." The author succeeds in transporting the reader to Thomas's sightless world, which is so rich in sensory observation. This unique book helps children understand what it is like to be blind.

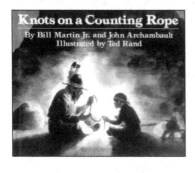

Knots on a Counting Rope

By Bill Martin Jr. and John Archambault. Illustrated by Ted Rand. Henry Holt, 1987.

During a stormy night a baby boy was born frail and weak. It did not seem he would survive. Two blue horses galloped by and gave the baby their strength, and the boy thrived despite his blindness. Around a glowing campfire Grandfather tells his grandson, Boy-Strength-of-Blue-Horses, the story of his birth and life in their North American Indian community. Each time Grandfather tells this story, he puts a knot in a counting rope. When the rope is filled, the boy will know the story by heart. This Reading Rainbow selection beautifully depicts intergenerational love and the strength to triumph over obstacles.

Keep Your Ear on the Ball

By Genevieve Petrillo. Illustrated by Lea Lyon. Tilbury House, 2007.

"Thanks, but no thanks" is Davey's response to every classmate's offer of help in this true story. Davey is blind, and he works hard to protect his independence. He is able to do almost everything his classmates can do without assistance, but the game of kickball presents significant difficulties. Respecting Davey's desire for independence, his classmates figure out how they can help. If they are quiet, Davey can listen for the ball and know when to kick. If they call out "first base, first base," Davey can listen and know where to run. This story is a wonderful demonstration of the value of interdependence.

My Buddy

By Audrey Osofsky. Illustrated by Ted Rand. Henry Holt, 1992.
Buddy is the service dog of a school-age boy with muscular dystrophy. Buddy can do things the boy cannot, such as turn the lights on and off, retrieve books, and bring the phone to the boy in his wheelchair. All these things help the boy be independent. The boy is concerned that people at school might not like Buddy, but his fellow students and his teacher quickly adjust and enjoy having Buddy around. Buddy shows us what daily life is like for the owner of a working dog and how rich and rewarding that life can be.

Anna and Natalie

By Barbara H. Cole. Illustrated by Ronald Himler. Star Bright, 2007.
Anna's class is taking a field trip to the Tomb of the Unknown Soldier, and four students will be selected for a special honor. These students will be chosen based on a persuasive letter they write for their teacher. Anna wants this honor very badly and talks to Natalie about the contest. The reader doesn't realize until the end of the book that Natalie is Anna's Seeing Eye dog, underscoring how highly able Anna is. Anna's blindness could be considered a secondary theme of this story.

Dad and Me in the Morning

By Patricia Lakin. Illustrated by Robert G. Steele. Albert Whitman, 1994.
A special alarm clock awakens Jacob in the predawn hours. Quietly, without disturbing the rest of the family, he wakes up his dad so that they can walk to the beach together to see the sunrise. They use lipreading, sign language, and hand squeezes to communicate with each other, and they enjoy sharing the things they see on their outing. The watercolor illustrations are highly effective in showing not only the change in lighting as time passes but also the endearing relationship between father and son.

Can You Hear a Rainbow?
The Story of a Deaf Boy Named Chris

By Jamee Riggio Heelan. Illustrated by Nicola Simmonds. Peachtree, 2002.
This nonfiction work mixes photographs with painting to tell the story of what life is like for Chris, a child who was born deaf. Chris has learned to read lips, speak, and use sign language to communicate with everyone, including his dog, who recognizes sign language commands. He attends public school with his siblings and has a number of friends that he has met through school, drama, and soccer. Chris observes that his deafness is just a minor difference between him and his friends, and, like a preference in sports, it doesn't hinder his relationships.

Some Kids Are Deaf

By Lola M. Schaefer. Illustrated with photographs. Capstone, 2008.
This nonfiction book written with simple text describes children who are deaf and shows some of their special needs. Chapters include "Deafness," "Tools for Hearing," "Talking," and "Everyday Life." A glossary defines terms that young readers may not know, such as *cochlear implant, sign language,* and *speech therapist.* Colorful photographs support the text and help the reader to comprehend the information presented. Suggested titles and Internet sites for further reading are included. This is a good choice for young readers or listeners who want an introduction to the topic.

Susan Laughs

By Jeanne Willis. Illustrated by Tony Ross. Henry Holt, 2000.
In charming illustrations and rhyming text, we meet Susan, a playful and spunky young girl. Preschoolers will relate to the activities and emotions Susan experiences, such as swinging, laughing, and being scared. Only at the very end of the story will they discover that Susan does all these things while in a wheelchair. This short book, accessible to even the youngest audience, focuses on abilities rather than disabilities.

Moses Goes to School

By Isaac Millman. Illustrated by the author. Farrar Straus Giroux, 2000.
It is the first day of school for Moses, who attends a public school in New York City for children who are deaf and hard of hearing. The students use American Sign Language (ASL) to communicate with one another, but

they also learn to read and write in English. Diagrams show how to sign common words and the song "Take Me Out to the Ball Game." Millman's introductory note explains how to read the diagrams and discusses the many ways that deaf children are so very similar to their hearing counterparts.

Best Friend on Wheels

By Debra Shirley. Illustrated by Judy Stead.
Albert Whitman, 2008.

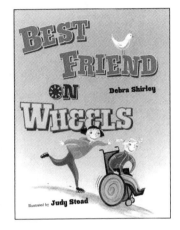

A girl is best friends with Sarah, and they like many of the same things. They both enjoy drawing cartoons, dancing, and hearing scary stories. When first introduced to Sarah at school, however, the girl is nervous because Sarah is in a wheelchair. The chair makes her seem quite different. But after discovering that both she and Sarah collect rocks, the girl is able to overcome her initial anxiety and find other commonalities. The rhyming text and humorous illustrations show that a disability is just one aspect of a whole person, and when someone focuses on other aspects, the disability fades into the background and becomes inconsequential to a relationship.

19

Divorce

NE OF THE MOST DISRUPTIVE, EMOTIONALLY TRAUMATIC situations children can experience is the divorce of their parents. Children dealing with divorce may feel alone, sad, angry, and worried about their future. Inspired books can confirm the universality of their feelings and predicament as well as help them anticipate and feel comfortable about the future.

In the books in this chapter, parents break up, get divorced, and remarry. Use these stories to open channels of communication with children. A child's comfort level in asking questions and sharing feelings directly affects his or her ability to make sense of and accept new family situations.

Living with Mom and Living with Dad

By Melanie Walsh. Illustrated by the author. Candlewick, 2012.
Large, colorful, lift-the-flap pages encourage child participation as a young girl compares the similarities and differences of life with each of her parents. The walls are not the same color in her two bedrooms, but both Mom

and Dad provide a night-light because they know she doesn't like the dark. Readers can view the differences between each of her safe and loving environments by lifting the flaps. The sturdy paper should hold up to repeated readings and flap flipping. This choice is well suited for children whose parents have separated or those trying to understand nontraditional living arrangements.

I Don't Want to Talk about It

By Jeanie Franz Ransom. Illustrated by Kathryn Kunz Finney. Magination, 2000.

The wide range of emotions a child might experience while going through a divorce is expressed in metaphors of wild animals. Lovely, large illustrations will capture the interest of young, animal-loving readers. Understanding parents are patient with their daughter's refusal to talk until she finally finds her voice and raises her concerns. Reassurance of their unwavering love and promises that some family traditions will remain comfort her. An in-depth note to parents, endorsed by the American Psychological Association, explains how to help a child of any age make a healthy adjustment to divorce.

Change Is Okay with Kacie Shay

By Jolie Carpenter. Illustrated by Lina Safar. Signature, 2010.

Charming watercolor illustrations and short rhyming text keep this story lighthearted. Kacie's mom and dad have a fairy-tale-like beginning, but when Kacie is a young girl, her parents announce that "Dad will be moving to live in a different house." At first, Kacie is worried that everything will change for the worse, but she quickly learns that life continues and even improves. The final text reads, "Things worked out fine and dandy, nobody was blue. And if you are ever in her shoes, you'll be just fine too!" This story is fitting for both separation and divorce, as the word *divorce* is never used.

Mama and Daddy Bear's Divorce

By Cornelia Maude Spelman. Illustrated by Kathy Parkinson. Albert Whitman, 1998.

Simple language and adorably illustrated bears make this selection a good choice for preschool kids. The family arranges for the bear siblings to live at Mama's house during the week and visit Daddy Bear's house on weekends.

The youngest bear misses the parent she is not with, but notices that her favorite belongings stay with her. This knowledge comforts her as she realizes that not everything has changed. The realization that everyone still loves her relieves much of her sadness. This book is honest in addressing some of the upsetting emotions and circumstances kids experience in divorced families.

Mom and Dad Glue

By Kes Gray. Illustrated by Lee Wildish. Barron's Educational Series, 2009.
Playful rhymes depict a young boy who initially feels responsible for his parents' breakup and thinks he can fix their relationship if he finds the right glue. Illustrations show a world with nearly everything broken, spotlighting how the emotions brought up by divorce are so difficult for children. The glue shop owner explains "That sometimes life works out this way, / That what must be must be." The boy then comes to terms with the finality of his parents' separation, assured that it won't affect their love for him.

My Parents Are Divorced, My Elbows Have Nicknames, and Other Facts about Me

By Bill Cochran. Illustrated by Steve Björkman. HarperCollins, 2009.
Having nicknames for his elbows or sleeping with one sock off doesn't make Ted weird. Feeling sad about his parents' divorce and the changes the divorce has brought to his life doesn't make him weird either. Ted is doing well adjusting to living at two houses and having a new stepmother. Full of personality, Ted humorously shares the facts and feelings of his life. Although having divorced parents is not what he would choose, he is coping well. Cartoonlike illustrations extend the humorous text, making this a strong choice for sharing with children who are navigating divorce.

Was It the Chocolate Pudding?
A Story for Little Kids about Divorce

By Sandra Levins. Illustrated by Bryan Langdo. Magination, 2005.
Written in the voice of a young boy thinking about his parents' divorce, this longer story has strong kid appeal. The boy is concerned that he

brought about his parents' divorce by causing them to argue when he made a mess with the chocolate pudding. He describes his daily life in two households, staying mainly at Dad's and going to his mother's some weekends. His mother tells him the divorce wasn't his fault, it was about "grown-up problems," and he immediately feels relieved. A "Note to Parents" discusses the emotional reactions of children faced with divorce, gives advice for explaining separation and divorce, and offers suggestions for helping children cope.

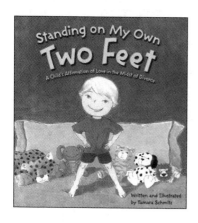

Standing on My Own Two Feet: A Child's Affirmation of Love in the Midst of Divorce

By Tamara Schmitz. Illustrated by the author. Price Stern Sloan, 2008.

Addison is quite accepting of the fact that he has two homes, one with Mom and one with Dad. He knows he is safe in both places and loved by both parents. It has been made clear to him that the divorce was not his fault. He is very confident and comfortable talking about the divorce and his certainty that he is deeply loved. The author uses simple sentences to create a matter-of-fact yet very positive mood. Young children will enjoy the bright illustrations of Addison's world and understand the basic and effective text.

On the Day His Daddy Left

By Eric J. Adams and Kathleen Adams. Illustrated by Layne Johnson. Albert Whitman, 2000.

In this story suitable for older children, the main character is a school-age boy. On a piece of paper, he writes a secret question that has clearly been bothering him: "Is it my fault?" When he shows this to his mother, she takes the paper, writes "NO," and instructs him to keep the paper with him always. He does, and he reads his question and his mother's answer daily. Eventually, he believes her answer but continues to ask questions about why his father left. The story has a comforting mood, and clear emotions are expressed in the pictures. In an afterword, the authors offer advice about talking to children about divorce.

Two Homes

By Claire Masurel. Illustrated by Kady MacDonald Denton. Candlewick, 2001.
Alex's mommy and daddy live in different places, but Alex has a room in each of their houses. Alex has two front doors and two favorite chairs. Friends come over to play at both houses. Alex loves Daddy, and Alex loves Mommy, and of course both Mommy and Daddy love Alex wherever Alex is staying. It is not clear whether Alex is a boy or a girl, making the character easy to identify with for everyone. Sweet illustrations of both of Alex's homes reassure readers that happiness and love can be found at two locations.

Oliver at the Window

By Elizabeth Shreeve. Illustrated by Candice Hartsough McDonald. Front Street, 2009.
Oliver starts at a new preschool when his parents separate. Although the new school has piles of blocks and a puppet-show stage, Oliver doesn't care. He just holds his stuffed lion and stands at the window waiting to see if it will be Mom or Dad who picks him up. As time passes and the seasons change, Oliver spends less and less time at the window. He enjoys his school friends and activities instead. When he has almost forgotten about the window, he sees a new student there crying. Oliver engages her, and she quickly joins the classroom activities.

My Mom's Wedding

By Eve Bunting. Illustrated by Lisa Papp. Sleeping Bear, 2006.
Pinky is excited to be the ring bearer in her mother's upcoming wedding, but she struggles with her feelings for her future stepdad. She feels guilty that she likes him almost as much as she likes her father and still hopes that her parents will get back together. With help from her father she finally accepts that her parents are now just friends and will not remarry. Pinky then understands that it is okay to love both of her dads. Papp effectively conveys each family member's feelings in snapshot-like, soft watercolor illustrations.

Sam's New Friend

By Thierry Robberecht. Illustrated by Philippe Goossens. Clarion, 2007.
Sam is a puppy who thinks that boys are tough and girls are not. Then Sam's mom invites the new girl home after school. Ellie is her friend's

daughter, and the little kitten is quiet and sad. Sam tries to comfort her and soon learns why Ellie is sad—her parents may be getting a divorce. Sam plays with his new friend at school the next day and doesn't mind when the other boys stare. Ellie doesn't know what will happen with her parents, but Sam knows she will be all right because Ellie is tough and brave, just like him.

20

Bullying

TEASING IS SOMETHING THAT ALMOST EVERY CHILD EXPERI-ences. It may be as innocent as playful joking with a friend, or it can cross the line if it becomes repetitive and feels unkind. Bullying behavior can be verbal or physical. It is characterized by a conscious and repetitive attempt to hurt another child. Adults can help children learn social skills for handling teasing, as well as positive ways to stand up for themselves and others. Children should also understand that it is important to let a responsible adult know if bullying is occurring. In this chapter, we recommend picture books that will be helpful for learning to deal with a variety of teasing and bullying situations.

How Full Is Your Bucket? For Kids
By Tom Rath and Mary Reckmeyer. Illustrated by Maurie J. Manning. Gallup Press, 2009.
Felix learns how his words and actions affect both himself and others, as his grandfather explains the concept of a full versus an empty bucket.

Everyone has a bucket that gets filled by kind words and deeds and emptied by unkindness. Told in a style that a young child can grasp and an older child will appreciate, the engaging story and illustrations deliver the timeless message of the golden rule. An adaptation of the number one best seller for adults, this picture book is a wonderful read-aloud for both the classroom and the home.

One

By Kathryn Otoshi. Illustrated by the author. KO Kids, 2008.
One person can make a difference when it comes to bullying. This creative tale uses colors and numbers to deliver the message that standing up for oneself and reaching out to others can have positive effects for everyone. Teaching acceptance and an appreciation for diversity in a deceptively simple story, this award-winning picture book is an excellent choice for a read-aloud at the start of the school year or whenever teasing crosses the line into bullying.

Chrysanthemum

By Kevin Henkes. Illustrated by the author. Greenwillow, 1991.
Chrysanthemum is proud of her name until she starts kindergarten. When Victoria and others make a mean-spirited game of teasing her about her unusual name, she turns to her loving parents for comfort. The tide finally turns when the class learns that their popular music teacher has quite an unusual name herself—Delphinium. Furthermore, she also plans to name her expected baby after Chrysanthemum. The class learns that being unique is a good thing after all. The charming illustrations and story will be sure to comfort a child dealing with similar issues.

Stop Picking on Me: A First Look at Bullying

By Pat Thomas. Illustrated by Lesley Harker. Barron's Educational Series, 2000.
Bullying behavior and its effects are explored in this sensitive informational picture book for children. Written by a psychotherapist and counselor, the book explains the issues surrounding bullying in simple terms to

promote conversation about the topic with young children. This book is part of a series of "first look" informational books on sensitive issues.

Just Kidding

By Trudy Ludwig. Illustrated by Adam Gustavson. Tricycle, 2005.
D.J. is teased and made fun of by his friend Vince. Every time Vince says something hurtful, he follows it with the explanation "Just kidding!" D.J. feels helpless and frustrated until he talks the problem through with his father. His father explains that Vince is acting this way because of something that is going on with him. D.J.'s brother and father give him a few strategies for dealing with kids who pick on others this way. Father and son also meet with the teacher, and together they come up with a plan to help Vince learn the consequences of his behavior. A foreword provides helpful advice for educators and parents, and a page of teasing dos and don'ts will be useful for kids.

Nobody Knew What to Do: A Story about Bullying

By Becky Ray McCain. Illustrated by Todd Leonardo. Albert Whitman, 2001.
Ray is being picked on by a group of bullies at school, and his classmates feel powerless to help. It gets so bad that Ray doesn't come to school, and a friend overhears the bullies plotting to do something even worse when he returns. Ray's friend decides to confide in a favorite teacher who always listens. The teacher reassures the friend that he did the right thing by telling her, and caring adults in the school resolve the situation with the children. A picture book for the intermediate grades, this realistic fiction story explores empowering ways to address physical and verbal bullying with adult intervention.

The Recess Queen

By Alexis O'Neill. Illustrated by Laura Huliska-Beith. Scholastic Press, 2002.
Mean Jean rules the playground until one day, spunky little Katie Sue arrives. She's the new kid who doesn't know the rules. After taking the lead in playground fun in a way that infuriates Mean Jean, Katie Sue has the audacity to ask Jean to play, something none of her classmates has ever

done! Told in rollicking prose with illustrations to match, this playful tale illustrates the power of one person standing up and reaching out. It makes an excellent companion piece to *One* by Kathryn Otoshi.

The Bully Blockers Club

By Teresa Bateman. Illustrated by Jackie Urbanovic. Albert Whitman, 2004.

Lotty Raccoon is looking forward to the start of school until she encounters Grant Grizzly, who bullies her relentlessly from day one. Lotty finally tells her parents and the teacher, but Grant continues to find ways to bully her when adults aren't looking. Finally, Lotty comes up with the solution: a Bully Blockers Club. Told with a sense of humor and a problem-solving approach, this empowering tale provides opportunities for a discussion of Lotty's changing emotions as she takes steps to solve the problem. As an added bonus, the book includes a page of information for adults.

Stand Tall, Molly Lou Melon

By Patty Lovell. Illustrated by David Catrow. G. P. Putnam's Sons, 2001.

Molly Lou Melon is the shortest girl in first grade, with unshakable self-confidence instilled by her equally tiny and confident grandma. When she has to move and attend a new school, the school bully immediately points out her "faults" as a tiny, funny-looking little girl. Undaunted, Molly Lou makes him look foolish as she proves again and again that she can do anything she sets her mind to. The comic illustrations and upbeat prose combine to make this an engaging choice for discussing the importance of believing in yourself and striving to be the best person you can be.

Sneaky Weasel

By Hannah Shaw. Illustrated by the author. Knopf, 2008.

Sneaky Weasel invites his friends to a big party to celebrate how rich he has become from his shady business scams. He is surprised and angry when nobody comes and sets out to confront his friends and demand an explanation. Weasel then discovers his bullying behavior has consequences, and he sets out to right his many wrongs and even do the unthinkable: to say he's sorry! This is a creative tale with a timeless message, and the text and art will be engaging for both primary and intermediate children.

The Orange Shoes

By Trinka Hakes Noble. Illustrated by Doris Ettlinger. Sleeping Bear, 2007.
Delly is a poor yet happy child with a loving family. Then her teacher tells the class about a Shoebox Social to raise money for art supplies. Although he can barely afford it, Delly's father buys her a new pair of shoes for the event. Delly wears them to school and is bullied by a mean group of girls, leaving her new shoes scuffed and scratched. Though heartbroken, she solves the problem by decorating painting flowers and vines on the damaged shoes. This warm, sensitive story illustrates the power of love and of staying true to oneself.

21

Death of a Parent or Loved One

COPING WITH THE DEATH OF A PARENT OR LOVED ONE IS DIFFI-cult at any age. Children especially need the support of caring adults during this time. Many adults, however, may find themselves uncomfortable talking about death or grieving themselves. Fortunately, there are excellent picture books that can serve as a bridge of communication between adult and child. Reading picture books together provides a comforting way for adults to help children understand and adjust to the loss. The books can provide a much-needed outlet for expressing thoughts and feelings, while focusing on the special memories of a loved one.

Always and Forever
By Alan Durant. Illustrated by Debi Gliori. Harcourt, 2004.
Mole, Fox, Otter, and Hare are the best of friends. They live together in a house in the woods and are a happy family. Then Fox becomes ill, and one day he goes into the woods alone and dies. His friends are deeply saddened and grieve together in their little house. Squirrel pays them a visit, and

they begin to share happy memories of Fox and what he meant to them all. The special memories help the animal friends get past their sadness. This gentle animal tale sends the comforting message that our loved ones stay in our hearts forever.

Bottled Sunshine

By Andrea Spalding. Illustrated by Ruth Ohi. Fitzhenry and Whiteside, 2005.

After spending a perfect summer holiday with his grandmother, Sammy is sad to leave. His grandmother comforts him by suggesting they "bottle some sunshine" that he can take home with him. Unsure of what this means, Sammy nevertheless sets out with his grandmother for one last adventure. They have a lovely day picking blackberries and making blackberry jam. Later that year, Sammy and his mother receive word that Grandma has passed away. He opens his precious jar and is comforted by loving memories. A touching story with gentle illustrations to match the tone, this book celebrates the love of a grandparent and grandchild.

One More Wednesday

By Malika Doray. Illustrated by the author. Translated from the French by Suzanne Freeman. Greenwillow, 2001.

A bunny tells of her special Wednesday visits with her granny. "On Wednesdays when I was little, Granny and I baked cakes and cookies. Then we ate them up." Charming line drawings embellish this sweet tale of love and loss. When Granny passes away, Papa frames a picture of Granny and the bunny to keep by her bed. The story ends on a comforting note, with the young bunny no longer feeling sad when she thinks of Granny, but instead remembering the happy days they spent together. This sweet story, simply told, is suitable for very young children.

Saying Goodbye to Daddy

By Judith Vigna. Illustrated by the author. Albert Whitman, 1991.

The day Clare's grandfather instead of her mother picks her up from school, Clare's whole world changes. Her mother and grandfather sadly explain that her father has died in an automobile accident. The story follows Clare as she attends the funeral and works through the grieving process with the help of her patient, kind grandfather, and loving, grieving mother. Young children coming to terms with a sudden death will be comforted by this gentle yet realistic story.

That Summer

By Tony Johnston. Illustrated by Barry Moser. Harcourt, 2002.
This is the moving story of two brothers, one of whom is dying from a terminal illness. The simple yet lyrical prose brings to life their last days together: "That summer moved like a dream quavering with heat and slow. All of us were dream walkers watching Joey." The boys struggle to come to terms with what is happening as the family draws closer together. Their grandmother teaches Joey how to quilt, and both boys gain solace from working precious memories into the pattern. The sensitive illustrations are a perfect complement to this inspirational story.

I Remember Miss Perry

By Pat Brisson. Illustrated by Stéphane Jorisch. Dial, 2006.
This poignant story deals with the sudden death of a beloved teacher. Stevie's teacher has made him feel special since his first day at the new school. She tells him that her fondest wish is to have lunch with him that day. As the year progresses, he learns that she has a daily fondest wish, and the class loves her for it. Then an accident occurs, and the children learn that Miss Perry has been in a fatal car crash. As the guidance counselor helps the students share their memories of Miss Perry, the children express their emotions and begin to heal.

Remembering Grandpa

By Uma Krishnaswami. Illustrated by Layne Johnson. Boyds Mills, 2007.
In this story of the power of treasured memories, Daysha helps her grandmother through a "bad case of sadness" a year after Grandpa's death. She gathers special items that remind her of him and takes her grandmother to see the collection she has placed in Grandpa's "special sunrise place." Grandma is touched and takes Daysha out for ice cream with sprinkles the way her grandfather used to do. Rabbits as characters instead of people, combined with lovely illustrations depicting springtime in the Southwest, may help some children more readily embrace the message in this healing tale.

Where Do People Go When They Die?

By Mindy Avra Portnoy. Illustrated by Shelly O. Haas. Kar-Ben, 2004.
In this thoughtful picture book, a child poses the title question to a variety of people, each time getting a different answer. The child eventually draws a conclusion: "They go to God. Who is everywhere." Answers are appropriate for young children, and the book offers helpful tips for parents when discussing death. Portnoy, a rabbi, takes a religious but nondenominational stance in the text and advice.

The Fall of Freddie the Leaf: A Story of Life for All Ages

By Leo Buscaglia. Illustrated with photographs. SLACK, 1982.
A beautifully told tale of a maple leaf experiencing the changes brought about by the seasons, this is a deceptively simple story of life's changes. As he grows, Freddie learns to appreciate what each season brings from his best friend, Daniel, the largest leaf on the tree. Daniel patiently explains how trees change and grow. Eventually fall arrives, and Freddie learns about the natural process of dying as he watches the other leaves turn brown and fall to the ground. This picture book provides a comforting look at nature to help understand death, especially for a young child experiencing loss.

I Miss You: A First Look at Death

By Pat Thomas. Illustrated by Lesley Harker. Barron's Educational Series, 2001.
The topic of death as a natural part of life is explored in this sensitive informational picture book for children. Written by a psychotherapist and counselor, the text explains the issues surrounding death in simple terms to promote conversation on the topic with young children. This book is part of a series by the author of "first look" informational books on sensitive issues.

Nana Upstairs and Nana Downstairs

By Tomie dePaola. Illustrated by the author. G. P. Putnam's Sons, 1998.
This classic story written by the beloved author and illustrator Tomie dePaola has been updated with new artwork. It tells the story of four-year-

old Tommy, who loves visiting his two grandmothers. Nana Upstairs, his great-grandmother, mostly stays in bed and always has candy mints for him. Nana Downstairs, his grandmother, lovingly cares for her grandson and her mother during Tommy's weekly visits. Both grandmothers eventually pass away as Tommy grows up. The loving tone expressed throughout this story makes it a timeless treasure to share with young children.

Where Is Grandpa?

By T. A. Barron. Illustrated by Chris K. Soentpiet. Philomel, 2000.
This autobiographical story tells of a boy remembering his grandfather and all they used to do together. The interplay of light and shadow in the illustrations helps evoke the tone as the story unfolds in the beautiful Rocky Mountains. The family gathers to share treasured stories about Grandpa, but the boy is unable to talk about his memories. He is finally comforted by his father's honest attempt to answer his question, "Where is Grandpa now?" A heartfelt depiction of a family coming to terms with their loss, this book is suitable for all elementary-age students.

Thank You, Grandpa

By Lynn Plourde. Illustrated by Jason Cockcroft. Dutton, 2003.
A little girl and her grandpa take nature walks together in this gentle story of love and loss. One day they come upon a dead grasshopper, and the girl's grandfather teaches her to say, "Thank you and good-bye" to the once-living creature. This becomes a shared ritual for them in their walks as the years pass, until finally one day the girl walks alone and offers this farewell to her grandfather. A touching story told with almost lyrical prose and softly hued illustrations, this book offers a unique way to cope with grief and loss.

City Dog, Country Frog

By Mo Willems. Illustrated by Jon J Muth. Hyperion, 2010.
City Dog is delighted to find himself in the country, free to run without a leash. He soon finds a new friend, Country Frog. Each season finds them playing together and teaching one another a new game. One fall day, Dog finds his friend, only to discover that Frog is too tired to explore and play. The two friends sit and play remembering games. Winter comes and Dog misses his friend. Spring arrives, and he makes a new friend, Country

Chipmunk. A touching, understated picture of friendship and loss, this is an excellent choice for sharing with children who have lost a friend through illness or moving.

22

Death of a Pet

THE DEATH OF A PET IS OFTEN A CHILD'S FIRST REAL EXPERI-ence with the inevitable end of life. Rather than dwelling on the sense of loss and grieving for an extended period of time, it is much healthier to celebrate the love and companionship the pet brought into the child's life. The books that follow show ingenious ways to help children focus on how much they enjoyed the life of their pet.

Desser the Best Ever Cat
By Maggie Smith. Illustrated by the author.
Knopf, 2001.
A school-age girl tells the story of her greatly loved and highly esteemed cat, Desser. Scrapbook-style illustrations help document Desser's life and support the text. We see Daddy finding Desser as a stray kitten and deciding to keep him, Desser in Dad's wedding photograph, and Desser adapting to a new baby in the house,

becoming part of busy family life, experiencing the ailments common to an old cat, and eventually passing away. The girl shows pictures of Desser to her new kitten while telling his story, modeling that it's healthy to share and appreciate memories while continuing to have happy pet relationships.

The Forever Dog

By Bill Cochran. Illustrated by Dan Andreasen. HarperCollins, 2007.
Corky is an oddly shaped dog, but Mike doesn't care; he and Corky are the very best of friends. They make a plan that they will be best friends forever. When Corky dies, Mike feels more hurt than he has ever felt before, but later becomes very angry because the Forever Plan is broken. Mike's mom helps him understand that the "Forever Plan was still going to work, only a little differently than he'd expected," because Corky can live in his heart forever. This warm and sensitive story will give children a tool for accepting their pet's death.

Goodbye Mousie

By Robie H. Harris. Illustrated by Jan Ormerod. Margaret K. McElderry, 2001.
A preschool-age boy wakes up to find his beloved pet mouse nonresponsive. Daddy explains that Mousie is dead, but the boy refuses to accept this and insists that Mousie will soon wake up. When the boy realizes that Mousie is indeed dead, he directs his anger at the animal. Then, through his sadness, he prepares and decorates a box for the burial of his cherished pet. By asking questions and expressing his feelings, the boy comes to accept Mousie's death. Readers will relate to this story and appreciate its helpfulness in coping with their own loss.

Dog Heaven

By Cynthia Rylant. Illustrated by the author. Blue Sky, 1995.
Newbery medalist Rylant gives a view of what living in Dog Heaven is like for our departed pets. Dogs run endlessly, eat creatively shaped dog biscuits, and play with loving angel children. They sleep nestled in clouds and can be escorted by angels on trips back to earth to visit their old homes. God watches out for these dogs and makes sure that heaven has everything to make them happy. Bright, childlike acrylic paintings aid in making this heaven seem a wonderful place, bringing comfort to those grieving and wondering about what happens to their dog after he dies.

The Best Cat in the World

By Lesléa Newman. Illustrated by Ronald Himler. Eerdmans, 2004.

Victor mourns the death of his beloved cat, Charlie. He sits at the cat's gravesite and becomes teary-eyed when talking about Charlie with his mother. When she suggests that they get a new cat, Victor is uninterested and states, "I don't want a new cat. I want Charlie." But a few weeks later the veterinarian calls and tells Victor that she has a kitten that needs a good home. Victor decides to adopt Shelley but finds that she is very different from Charlie. Nonetheless, Victor grows to love and appreciate Shelley for the wonderful cat that she is.

Jasper's Day

By Marjorie Blain Parker. Illustrated by Janet Wilson. Kids Can, 2002.

In this touching story, Jasper, an aged golden retriever, spends a celebration day with his family before being euthanized. Riley stays home from school so they can take Jasper to his favorite places, which include a stream, The Big Scoop ice cream shop, and Grandma's house. At day's end, Riley says good-bye to Jasper before Dad takes the dog to the vet to be put down. Riley realizes that Jasper is in pain and thinks, "Maybe Jasper is ready." This sad but realistic story celebrates a beloved pet's life and offers support for those facing a similar situation.

The Tenth Good Thing about Barney

By Judith Viorst. Illustrated by Erik Blegvad. Atheneum, 1971.

A little boy is sad when his cat, Barney, dies. His mother tells him to think of ten good things about Barney that he can say at Barney's funeral. The boy is only able to think of nine. The next day, while helping his father in the garden, he realizes that "in the ground everything changes." He also discovers the tenth good thing—that Barney will help the trees, flowers, and grass to grow, which is a "pretty nice job for a cat." Small black-ink drawings add to the gentle quietness of this story.

Saying Goodbye to Lulu

By Corinne Demas. Illustrated by Ard Hoyt. Little, Brown, 2004.

Lulu, a lovable, once-spunky dog, is growing old and weak. Her companion, a school-age girl, gives tender care but wants Lulu back "the way she used to be." When Lulu inevitably dies, the girl is deeply saddened. With the help of her parents she buries Lulu but cannot say good-bye, crying instead. Months later in spring, she finally accepts Lulu's death and is able to open her heart to a new puppy. This hopeful, honest story about a child experiencing the decline and death of a beloved pet is accessible and heartfelt.

When a Pet Dies

By Fred Rogers. Photographs by Jim Judkis. G. P. Putnam's Sons, 1988.

In his classic straightforward, comforting, and honest style, Rogers writes about the common feelings, such as frustration, sadness, and loneliness, that children experience when their pet dies. The reality is that sometimes, even when a pet has the best of care by its owner or by a veterinarian, it may be too sick, hurt, or old to live. Rogers encourages children to share their feelings and questions with their parents and reminds us all that there will come "a time when you can feel happy again about the good times you and your pet had together."

City Dog, Country Frog

By Mo Willems. Illustrated by Jon J Muth. Hyperion, 2010.

City Dog is delighted to find himself in the country, free to run without a leash. He soon finds a new friend, Country Frog. Each season finds them playing together and teaching one another a new game. One fall day, Dog finds his friend, only to discover that Frog is too tired to explore and play. The two friends sit and play remembering games. Winter comes and Dog misses his friend. Spring arrives, and he makes a new friend, Country Chipmunk. A touching, understated picture of friendship and loss, this is an excellent choice for sharing with children who have lost a friend through illness or moving.

Remembering Crystal

By Sebastian Loth. Illustrated by the author. NorthSouth, 2010.

Zelda the goose and Crystal the turtle are best pals. They do everything together—read books, swim, take trips, and talk about life. However, Crystal is growing old. One day Zelda does not find Crystal in her usual spot. Zelda's friends tell her that the turtle has died. At first Zelda refuses to believe this and goes on an exhaustive search. Unsuccessful, Zelda realizes the truth and comes to accept that Crystal will be with her always through her memories of their shared experiences. The earth-toned and charmingly simple illustrations provide lightness and humor to a difficult topic.

23

Mother Nature

OTHER NATURE GIVES US BEAUTIFUL DAYS, WITH sunshine and rain to help grow flowers, vegetables, and trees. Weather can be a source of wonder and fascination, but sometimes harsh weather can cause concern. By sharing stories that describe natural phenomena such as hurricanes, tsunamis, tornadoes, and thunderstorms, children gain a better understanding of the nature of these events, and any misconceptions can be dispelled. By reading stories of perseverance and survival, children gain strength and courage. The books in this collection also explain how to prepare for emergencies and provide tips on staying safe. Many of the books include definitions of key weather terms.

A Place Where Hurricanes Happen

By Renée Watson. Illustrated by Shadra Strickland. Random House, 2010.
Adrienne, Keesha, Michael, and Tommy are best friends. They play together often in their New Orleans neighborhood. In an alternating,

first-person format, each tells of friendship and survival in the face of Hurricane Katrina. The four friends describe their families and their interests prior to the storm—Michael likes to draw pictures, and Keesha makes jambalaya with her mother. The storm approaches, and each child shares how his or her family prepares. Finally, the children tell of Katrina's aftermath and life's disruption endured, but they do not let the hurricane define their home city of New Orleans.

Two Bobbies: A True Story of Hurricane Katrina, Friendship, and Survival

By Kirby Larson and Mary Nethery. Illustrated by Jean Cassels. Walker, 2008.

In this hopeful story that will appeal to survivors of natural disasters, Bobbi, a medium-sized dog, and Bob Cat, a white-and-orange cat, help each other through the devastation after Hurricane Katrina. Deserted in flooded New Orleans, Bobbi and Bob Cat wander the streets for months in search of food and water. Finally, at a construction worksite, a man cares for them and brings them to an animal shelter. At the shelter workers discover that Bob Cat is blind and Bobbi is his Seeing Eye dog. After TV exposure, the two animals are permanently adopted into a loving home.

A Mama for Owen

By Marion Dane Bauer. Illustrated by John Butler. Simon and Schuster, 2007.

The true story of a young hippo that was separated from his mother during the 2004 Indian Ocean tsunami has captured the attention of many people around the world. In this version of the story, the young hippo, Owen, sleeps, eats, and plays with his mother until they are separated in the flooded Sabaki River and washed out to sea. A panicked Owen is washed ashore and finds Mzee, an old tortoise that looks like his momma. Mzee and Owen become inseparable companions. An author's note provides factual information about the real Owen and Mzee.

Hurricanes!

By Gail Gibbons. Illustrated by the author. Holiday House, 2009.

Using colorful and detailed illustrations, this nonfiction book gives a general overview of hurricanes. The book explains how hurricanes form and includes concepts such as evaporation, condensation, updraft, and eye formation. The Saffir-Simpson scale and Category 1–5 impacts such as wind speed, storm surge, and possible destruction are discussed. The book also provides information on where hurricanes form, where they strike, which hurricanes have been the worst in the United States, and how hurricanes are forecast. The straightforward text gives definitions for key terms often used when talking about hurricanes and provides safety instructions for hurricane preparedness.

Tornadoes!

By Gail Gibbons. Illustrated by the author.
Holiday House, 2009.

Gibbons once again does an outstanding job of simply explaining a natural phenomenon. Using illustrations that incorporate the terminology and definitions associated with tornadoes, the author describes the formation, classification, and potential destruction of tornadoes. The text defines each of the five levels of the Enhanced Fujita Tornado Damage Scale and illustrates the expected destruction for each. Gibbons discusses the two most destructive tornado levels and lets kids know how they can stay safe by providing instructions in a chapter titled "What to Do When a Tornado Approaches."

Dinosaur Thunder

By Marion Dane Bauer. Illustrated by Margaret Chodos-Irvine. Scholastic
Press, 2012.

Brannon is horribly afraid of thunder. Whenever a loud bang, boom, or crack sounds from the sky, he runs and hides. His family provides many different explanations for the thunder. His father suggests the thunder is a "big cat purring." Brannon considers this, until the next clap of thunder comes, causing him to hide behind the couch. Many more explanations are given, but none assuages his fear until his brother whispers that it is only dinosaurs stomping around. Brannon knows all about dinosaurs and decides to accept the thunder as something exciting. Colorful collage illustrations enhance the story.

Rain Play

By Cynthia Cotten. Illustrated by Javaka Steptoe. Henry Holt, 2008.
Usually when it rains people run for cover, not wanting to get wet. Not so for the group of African American children playing in the park in this story. Instead they enjoy the feeling of the rain as it cools their skin, play in the puddles, and collect rain in cups made out of leaves. When lightning streaks across the sky and thunder booms, the children quickly leave for home but still watch the storm until its finish. Painted collage paper and sparse rhyming verse that rollicks right along make this book perfect for the toddler crowd.

Catty Jane, Who Hated the Rain

By Valeri Gorbachev. Illustrated by the author. Boyds Mills, 2012.
Catty Jane, a kitten, is scared of thunder and lightning and refuses to do anything when it rains. When her rain-loving friends Piggy, Froggy, and Goose come over, they suggest doing fun, rainy-day activities. Catty Jane, who does not want to get wet or be outside when it's raining, refuses. Her friends then decide to throw a rainy-day party, and after some convincing Catty Jane agrees to give it a try. By the time the rain stops, Catty Jane has overcome her fear of getting wet and enjoys splashing in puddles with her friends.

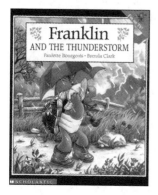

Franklin and the Thunderstorm

By Paulette Bourgeois. Illustrated by Brenda Clark. Scholastic, 1998.
Franklin checks the thermometer and barometer every day because he is worried about the weather. Even though the dark sky and ominous clouds make Franklin feel jumpy inside, he walks over to Fox's house to play. Beaver, Snail, and Hawk join their play and don't mind being outside with a storm approaching. When rain begins to fall, Fox's mother insists they come inside. Franklin's friends ease his concerns with silly weather stories and true explanations of weather phenomena. Children will relate to this ever-popular character and will be happy to see him successfully combat his fear of storms.

The Big Storm: A Very Soggy Counting Book

By Nancy Tafuri. Illustrated by the author. Simon and Schuster, 2009.

As the sky turns gray and dark clouds gather, ten woodland animals run into a hill hollow to seek refuge from the thunderstorm. There is room for everyone, including Squirrel, Mouse, Raccoon, and even Skunk. The animals wait out the harsh weather, but when the storm has cleared they still hear "a rumble and a grumble in the air." Surprise! Two bears are in the hollow, too. One by one the animals flee to find a very beautiful day. Tafuri's large illustrations are spectacular and, combined with simple text and a counting theme, make this work a toddler winner.

The Bears in the Bed and the Great Big Storm

By Paul Bright. Illustrated by Jane Chapman. Good Books, 2008.

As Bear and Mrs. Bear sleep soundly in their bed, outside the wind whirls and a thunderstorm develops. One by one Baby Bear, Little Bear, and then Young Bear, afraid of the storm's sounds and monsterlike shadows, join them in bed. When the monster turns out to be a moose looking for shelter, the bears all have a good laugh at their foolishness. The book's large size and adorable illustrations are child pleasing. Children will likely identify with the young bears' fears and be comforted by the story's conclusion.

Ohio Thunder

By Denise Dowling Mortensen. Illustrated by Kate Kiesler. Clarion, 2006.

The cornstalks are high on the Ohio plains when a thunderstorm comes rolling through. Using rhythmic couplets Mortensen creates the feel of a fierce hail-producing storm as it speedily moves over a rural family farm. Taking cover in a red-roofed barn, Dad and his two boys watch the remarkable storm with their dog. The drama of the wind, rain, thunder, lightning, and even hail is fully realized in the illustrations before the sky brightens as the storm moves on. The drama concludes with an eye toward a fresh rainbow and the coming harvest.

Hooray for Summer!

By Kazuo Iwamura. Illustrated by the author. NorthSouth, 2010.

In this lively story a hot summer's day quickly turns into a dreary rainy afternoon. The squirrel children Mick, Mack, and Molly are outside playing until a dark rain cloud appears. As they run to take cover, the rain begins. Happily they find a cave that is already occupied by two very timid mice. A rabbit soon joins them, and together they wait out the storm. When the weather clears, many animals come out from hiding and enjoy the cooler air. Two-page muted illustrations express the animals' emotions during the changing weather events of the day.

24

God, Spirituality, and Awe of Life

MANY PARENTS VIEW EDUCATING THEIR CHILDREN about God, spirituality, or divine inspiration as their responsibility. Books about God or spirituality can introduce children to the sense of awe and wonder about the nature of life. They begin to understand that there are forces or energies greater than themselves. As with language skills, social and emotional development, and other areas of early learning, young children depend on caring adults to help them grow and become their best selves. One of the challenges of this topic was to find books that are nondenominational and universally inspiring. Learning about God, the awe of life, or whatever spiritual or philosophical concept a family chooses lends itself to learning about morals and ethics.

Old Turtle

By Douglas Wood. Illustrated by Cheng-Khee Chee. Scholastic Press, 2007.
Old Turtle, originally published in 1992, celebrates the wonders of creation.

Long ago, the wise oracle, Old Turtle, helped to dispel the arguing and negativity among the rocks, the trees, the birds, the animals, and the oceans about who or what God is. The message of connectivity among all things and all beings is magnanimous. Adults and children will enjoy this simple but powerful fable.

Where Is God?

By Lawrence and Karen Kushner. Illustrated by Dawn W. Majewski. Skylight Paths, 2000.

Young children have a strong, innate capacity to know God. Popular author Rabbi Kushner and his wife, Karen, create a doorway into the realm of spiritual reality and possibility. They depict simple yet meaningful events for young children. Parents can use the joy of cookies fresh from the oven, the magic of the family's new baby, and the gentleness of Grandmother as she grows old to help children discover that God is everywhere. Majewski captures the beauty of these everyday activities in bright watercolors. This nondenominational approach presents children with an understanding of how to connect to divine energy and celebrate life.

Buddha

By Demi. Illustrated by the author. Henry Holt, 1996.

Award-winning author and illustrator Demi portrays the transformational journey of Siddhartha from a young prince into the Buddha. Although the text is for older children, the stunning beauty and colorful detail of the artwork will intrigue children of all ages. Parents can summarize and highlight the story as needed. Reading and reflecting on Buddha's teachings refresh the soul and help one let go of "bad thoughts and [keep] good ones."

Arrow to the Sun: A Pueblo Indian Tale

By Gerald McDermott. Illustrated by the author. Viking, 1974.

This folktale magnifies humans' desire to draw on the power of the universal mind or the Sun to clarify life's purpose. McDermott won a Caldecott Medal for his portrayal of a boy's quest to find his father, the Lord of the Sun, and bring his spirit to Earth. Through trial and error the boy finds assistance from the wise Arrow Maker. Bravely passing several tests posed by the Sun, the boy succeeds in bringing love, wisdom, and goodwill to the human world. The warm reds, oranges, and yellows enliven the geometric illustrations of American native culture.

The Easter Story

By Brian Wildsmith. Illustrated by the author. Knopf, 1994.
Jesus's final days on earth, universally known as the Easter story, are outlined in this vibrant rendition for young children. Award-winning Wildsmith splendidly tells the story through the eyes of Jesus's donkey. The little donkey holds his head high as he and Jesus enter Jerusalem. He keenly observes Jesus throughout the story, during all the major events: the Last Supper, the Agony in the Garden of Gethsemane, the arrest of Jesus, the Crucifixion, and the Resurrection. The donkey returns home and remembers "the kind and good man" who rode on his back to Jerusalem.

Images of God for Young Children

By Marie-Hélène Delval. Illustrated by Barbara Nascimbeni. Eerdmans, 2010.

Families can use *Images of God* as a springboard for discussions of spirituality. God is described in many ways—as light, wisdom, mercy, love, and joy. The colorful and expressive artwork masterfully presents illustrations to help children use their imaginations to think about the meaning of these qualities. The spring, a rock, a stream, and other natural elements are deftly used to help children ponder spirituality. The ending suggests that "God is within us" too. Many parents will also appreciate the representation of Jesus as the image of God in body and face.

Zen Shorts

By Jon J Muth. Illustrated by the author. Scholastic Press, 2005.
Some parents may find this story helpful. Stillwater, the giant panda, shows up in his neighbor's backyard and surprises the children—Addy, Michael, and Karl. Over the course of the next three days, each child takes a turn visiting Stillwater. They play and have fun together sitting in a tent, painting, flying paper airplanes, climbing trees, and swimming in the pool. Each day Stillwater tells a story for each child to think about and learn

from—Uncle Ry, who never lets anyone leave empty-handed; the farmer, who integrates the duality of life; and the monk, who does not carry the baggage of the past with him.

On Noah's Ark

By Jan Brett. Illustrated by the author. G. P. Putnam's Sons, 2003.
Best-selling author and illustrator Brett tells the marvelous biblical story of the ark through the eyes of Noah's granddaughter. The little girl takes the reader through building the ark, guiding the animals to squeeze on board, enduring the forty days of rain, and welcoming the burst of sunshine that signals it is time to settle on land once again. Brett researched the animals of Botswana in order to draw several mammals and birds in their natural settings. The resulting stunning illustrations will charm adults and children alike.

Afterword

A Tale of Two Books:
Peter Rabbit Meets the Count of Monte Cristo

THE COUNT OF MONTE CRISTO STROLLED UP THE LANE, ENJOY-ing the sound his rustling pages made in the gentle breeze. The sun's rays shone on his thick spine and heated his dark canvas jacket, making him perspire. He was puffed up with fame, and his title, like a chin, projected jauntily in the air.

"Excuse me, sir, can you tell me the way to fame and glory?" asked Peter Rabbit. "I wish to be read like you, far and wide, for years and years. I am only a small, slim volume, which very few readers take seriously," he continued.

"Is someone speaking to me?" bellowed the Count, who, being very upper shelf, did not recognize those he considered of lower status.

"Why, yes!" piped up Peter Rabbit. "I asked for your advice on getting fame and glory."

"Oh, it is advice you want. You are clever to ask one as great as I," the Count replied. Such requests stroked the Count's ego, so he offered, "First you need to drop your pictures. What value do silly drawings have?"

"No pictures! How will children be able to follow my story?" Peter Rabbit questioned.

"You asked for fame and glory, so do not be concerned with children," rebutted the Count. "Next, you are too skinny. You need to beef up; add words, I say, and lots of them. Fill yourself until your binding almost bursts."

"That sounds very uncomfortable; I'm not sure children will spend time with me if I grow that large," worried Peter Rabbit.

"Children, shmildren!" the Count roared in a literary rage. "Pray tell, why on earth do you continue to concern yourself with children? They cannot follow a complex story! They cannot appreciate epic proportion! The little squirmy ones can't even sit with you for any length of time!"

As Peter Rabbit dusted the Count's spittle off his jacket, he considered the Count's words. He suddenly realized that fame and glory were of no interest to him. His wish was to be held in the loving hands of a child, whose young eyes would light eagerly on his words and pictures. That was a much richer reward than fame and glory.

Books can open the door to learning for children—and to a greater understanding of life's lessons. They can lead families to have thoughtful discussions filled with optimism, compassion, and joy. A book can unlock the imagination of millions of readers. Each book is a doorway to the world of understanding, a tiny package of light sitting silently on the library shelf until we open it and let its light draw us, adults and children alike, into the world of knowing.

Resources

The books and websites in this section are only a few of the many resources to help parents further investigate tender topics and locate great books to share with their children.

BOOKS

What to Read When: The Books and Stories to Read with Your Child and All the Best Times to Read Them
Pam Allyn. Avery, 2009.

Best Books for Kids Who Think They Hate to Read
Laura Backes. Prima, 2001.

Touchpoints Birth to Three: Your Child's Emotional and Behavioral Development, revised edition
T. Berry Brazelton with Joshua Sparrow. Da Capo Lifelong, 2006.

Touchpoints Three to Six: Your Child's Emotional and Behavioral Development
T. Berry Brazelton and Joshua D. Sparrow. Perseus, 2001.

Read-Alouds with Young Children
R. Campbell. International Reading Association, 2001.

Read to Me: Raising Kids Who Love to Read
B. Cullinan. Scholastic, 1992.

Healing Stories: Picture Books for the Big and Small Changes in a Child's Life
Jacqueline Golding. M. Evans, 2006.

Raising an Emotionally Intelligent Child
John Gottman. Fireside, 1998.

Your Child's Growing Mind: Brain Development and Learning from Birth to Adolescence, third edition
Jane Healy. Three Rivers, 2004.

Seven Skills for School Success: Activities to Develop Social and Emotional Intelligence in Young Children
Pam Schiller. Gryphon House, 2009.

The Whole-Brain Child: 12 Revolutionary Strategies to Nurture Your Child's Developing Mind
Daniel Siegel. Delacorte, 2011.

Blackwell Handbook of Childhood Social Development
Edited by Peter K. Smith and Craig H. Hart. Blackwell, 2002.

The Read-Aloud Handbook, sixth edition
Jim Trelease. Penguin, 2006.

My Shining Star: Raising a Child Who Is Ready to Learn
Rosemary Wells. Scholastic, 2006.

WEBSITES

The Adventures of Everyday Geniuses
www.theadventuresofeverydaygeniuses.com
A companion site to the innovative series of children's books, this resource offers insight into the series' creation and mission to expose the broader definitions of learning, creativity, and intelligence in a child-friendly format. Each of the stories in the series introduces a learning style or learning difference, while offering realistic examples of triumph over difficulty.

American Academy of Pediatrics
www.aap.org
Dedicated to the health of all children, the American Academy of Pediatrics site provides a wealth of information about the mental and physical health of children and teens.

American Psychological Association
www.apa.org
Administered by the largest scientific and professional organization for psychology in the United States, this site provides authoritative information on psychology topics such as anger, anxiety, bullying, death and dying, depression, disability, and emotional health. Each topic is defined and includes additional links to related articles from CNN, the *New York Times,* and BBC News.

Center on the Social and Emotional Foundations for Early Learning
http://csefel.vanderbilt.edu
This national resource center disseminates research and evidence-based practices to early childhood programs across the country. The SEFEL website offers a treasure trove of free downloadable information on the social emotional development and school readiness of children, including a "Book Nook" page with titles and suggested extension activities.

Challenging Behavior
www.challengingbehavior.org
The Technical Assistance Center on Social Emotional Intervention for Young Children puts research into everyday practice. They use the pyramid

model as a conceptual framework to promote social-emotional competence and to address challenging behavior.

Children's Book Council

www.cbcbooks.org

The Children's Book Council is the nonprofit trade association of U.S. children's book publishers. The organization sponsors the Every Child a Reader initiative, which is dedicated to instilling a lifelong love of reading in children, as well as a national Children's Book Week.

Cooperative Children's Book Center

www.education.wisc.edu/ccbc/

The Cooperative Children's Book Center is part of the University of Wisconsin–Madison School of Education. They are the definitive experts in children's literature and offer annotated lists of award-winning books for all ages and interests.

Early Literacy Learning

www.earlyliteracylearning.org

The Center for Early Literacy Learning promotes the adoption and sustained use of evidence-based early literacy learning practices through easy-to-understand information and activity suggestions. This site is focused on guiding adults to help young children with identified disabilities and developmental delays.

Gesell Institute of Child Development

www.gesellinstitute.org

Gesell Institute programs, publications, and research efforts focus on educating and supporting teachers and parents in order to ensure the future success of all children through understanding the ages and stages of childhood. The institute has offered a variety of medical and educational programs and services to promote the healthy development of children and adults worldwide since 1950.

Helpguide

www.helpguide.org

Helpguide assists parents and professionals in navigating information about children's emotional problems, learning disorders, and other special needs. Helpguide collaborates with Harvard Health Publications, the consumer health publishing division of Harvard Medical School.

KidsHealth

http://kidshealth.org/parent/

A popular website for children's health and development, KidsHealth has three targeted audiences: parents, kids, and teens. Frequently asked questions are covered in several categories, including general health, growing up, emotions and behavior, parenting, safety, school, and sexual development.

Maryland Healthy Beginnings

www.marylandhealthybeginnings.org

Healthy Beginnings champions parents and caregivers of infants and toddlers to nurture the potential for learning and growth of young children. This colorful site gives information and support about child care and child development, including an Activity Planner with fun, developmentally appropriate activities that build young children's skills and promote all kinds of learning.

PBS Parents

www.pbs.org/parents/

PBS Parents provides information on important topics, such as child development and early learning. This engaging site also gives parents an insight into PBS KIDS, with its many learning games, shows, and age-appropriate activities.

Reading Rockets

www.readingrockets.org/audience/

This award-winning site offers a wealth of information on teaching children to read, including specific information on how to help struggling readers.

Ready At Five

www.readyatfive.org

Ready At Five is a self-sustaining, board-designated program of the Maryland Business Roundtable for Education focused on helping young children enter school with the skills they need to succeed. Their website offers free information and resources for parents, caregivers, librarians, and early childhood educators, including forty-four downloadable, hands-on activities to make learning fun.

Surviving Deployment

www.survivingdeployment.com
Surviving Deployment provides online information and resources for military families.

Zero to Three

www.zerotothree.org
Zero to Three is a national, nonprofit organization that promotes the health and development of infants and toddlers by targeting professionals, policy makers, and parents. The website features an interactive baby brain map that shows how early care enriches development.

About the Authors

Dorothy Stoltz is head of outreach services and programming for Carroll County (Maryland) Public Library. She is coauthor of *Every Child Ready for School: Helping Adults Inspire Young Children to Learn* (American Library Association, 2013). She has written and coauthored several articles on historic children's books, peer coaching, and immigrant services and has served on the Special Collections and Bechtel Fellowship Committee of the Association for Library Service to Children. She spearheaded a successful early literacy training, research-tested study and is project director for early literacy training, early literacy peer coaching, library programming, mobile services, community outreach, and several LSTA and other grant projects, including Parents as Teachers, at her library. She also oversees the statewide early literacy peer coaching wiki project. She is currently serving on the Every Child Ready to Read oversight committee of the Public Library Association and the Association for Library Service to Children. She received her MLS from Clarion University of Pennsylvania.

Elaine Czarnecki is a reading specialist and literacy consultant. She also teaches in the Graduate Reading Program at Johns Hopkins University.

She is coauthor of *Every Child Ready for School: Helping Adults Inspire Young Children to Learn* (American Library Association, 2013). She was the literacy consultant for a successful early literacy training study at Carroll County (Maryland) Public Library and is currently the literacy consultant for the library's early literacy peer coaching project. She serves as consultant and trainer for Maryland public libraries and has delivered early literacy training to library systems in Virginia, Pennsylvania, Minnesota, Wisconsin, and Washington State. Elaine has participated in curriculum development at both the county and state levels. She has served as an editor/consultant for Sadlier Publishing's Vocabulary series and as a language arts writer for Words and Numbers, Inc. She received her master of education degree from Loyola College in Baltimore, Maryland.

Buff Kahn is the children's services supervisor at the Eldersburg Branch of the Carroll County (Maryland) Public Library. More than fifty storytimes for children from birth to age five are offered each month at the Eldersburg Library in addition to many other programs for older children and teens. Buff enjoys presenting storytimes and is a lead coach for Carroll County Public Library's storytime peer coaching project. She was instrumental in the success of the project by modeling the effective implementation of peer coaching in a branch library. She received her MLS from the University of Maryland's College of Information Studies, where she was a 2006 recipient of the Dean's Award. Buff serves in the Maryland Library Association's Children's Services Division and helps train librarians statewide on peer coaching best practices.

Index

A

access to books, 4
Adams, Eric J., 126
Adams, Kathleen, 126
adoption, books about, 101–105
The Adventures of Everyday Geniuses
    (website), 161
Agassi, Martine, 53
Alborough, Jez, 54
Alda, Arlene, 82
Alfie's Attack (Bohline), 83–84
Aliki, 28, 93–94
Alimonti, Frederick, 62
All by Myself! (Aliki), 28
All Cats Have Asperger Syndrome
    (Hoopmann), 109
All the Colors of the Earth (Hamanaka),
    114
Allyn, Pam, 159
The Alphabet War (Robb), 108
Always and Forever (Durant), 135–136
America Is- (Borden), 39
American Academy of Pediatrics
    (website), 161
American Library Association (ALA), 13
American Psychological Association
    (website), 161
Andrew's Angry Words (Lachner), 44

Anna and Natalie (Cole), 119
Another Brother (Cordell), 72
Archambault, John, 118
Are You a Cow? (Boynton), 29
Armstrong, Jewel, 99–100
Arrow to the Sun (McDermott), 154–155
Asch, Frank, 39
Asperger syndrome, 107–110
Association for Library Service to
    Children (ALSC), 13
attention deficit hyperactivity disorder,
    107–110
Augustus and His Smile (Rayner), 31
autism, 107–110
awe of life, books about, 153–156

B

babies, books about, 66–72
Babies Don't Eat Pizza (Danzig), 66
Baby Baby Blah Blah Blah! (Shipton),
    66
Baby Baobab (Robinson), 40–41
Baby Faces (Miller), 49
Back into Mommy's Tummy
    (Robbrecht), 67
Backes, Laura, 159
A Bad Case of Tattle Tongue (Cook), 79
Bair, Sheila, 88

Balloons over Broadway (Sweet), 59
Bang, Molly, 12–13, 46
Banks, Kate, 60
Barrett, Mary Brigid, 74
Barretta, Gene, 58–59
Barron, T. A., 139
Bateman, Teresa, 132
Battersby, Katherine, 22
Bauer, Marion Dane, 148–149
Bawk and Roll (Sauer), 51
Be Careful and Stay Safe (Meiners),
    61–62
Bear Feels Scared (Wilson), 52
The Bears in the Bed (Bright), 151
Bears on Chairs (Parenteau), 18
Beatrice's Goat (McBrier), 89–90
Beaumont, Karen, 18
Bedtime for Frances (Hoban), 47
behavioral issues, books about, 107–110
Being Friends (Beaumont), 18
Berenstain, Stan and Jan, 23, 62, 87, 93
*The Berenstain Bears and the Trouble
    with Friends* (Berenstain and
    Berenstain), 23
*The Berenstain Bears Learn about
    Strangers* (Berenstain and
    Berenstain), 62
The Berenstain Bears' Moving Day
    (Berenstain and Berenstain),
    93
*The Berenstain Bears' Trouble with
    Money* (Berenstain and
    Berenstain), 87
*Best Books for Kids Who Think They
    Hate to Read* (Backes), 159
The Best Cat in the World (Newman),
    143
Best Friend on Wheels (Shirley), 121
Big Ernie's New Home (Martin and
    Martin), 92
Big Plans (Shea), 30
Big Sister Now (Sheldon), 68–69
The Big Storm (Tafuri), 151
Black, White, Just Right! (Davol), 114
The Black Book of Colors (Cottin), 118
Blackwell Handbook (Smith and Hart),
    160
Bohline, David, 83–84
Boomer's Big Day (McGeorge), 92

Borden, Louise, 39
Bottled Sunshine (Spalding), 136
Bourgeois, Paulette, 55, 150
Boxes for Katje (Fleming), 33–34
Boynton, Sandra, 26, 29
Brazelton, T. Berry, 159
Bread, Bread, Bread (Morris), 112–113
Brett, Jan, 156
Bright, Paul, 151
Brisson, Pat, 96, 137
Brown, Don, 58
Brown, Laurie Krasny, 20
Brown, Margaret Wise, 48
Brown, Peter, 18–19
Buddha (Demi), 154
The Bully Blockers Club (Bateman), 132
bullying, books about, 129–133
Bunting, Eve, 63, 96, 102, 127
Burningham, John, 67
Buscaglia, Leo, 138
But I Wanted a Baby Brother! (Feiffer), 69

C
Calm-Down Time (Verdick), 53
Campbell, R., 160
Can You Hear a Rainbow? (Heelan), 120
Carle, Eric, 52
Carpenter, Jolie, 124
Catty Jane, Who Hated Rain
    (Gorbachev), 150
Center on the Social and Emotional
    Foundations (website), 161
Challenging Behavior (website), 161–162
Change Is Okay with Kacie Shay
    (Carpenter), 124
Chester's Way (Henkes), 21
Children are the World (Montanari), 114
Children's Book Council (website), 162
A Child's Garden of Verses (Stevenson), 34
Christiansen, Rebecca, 99–100
Chrysanthemum (Henkes), 130
City Dog, Country Frog (Willems), 21,
    139–140, 144
Clark, Karen Henry, 102–103
Cocca-Leffler, Maryann, 87–88
Cochran, Bill, 125, 142
Cohen, Miriam, 99
Cole, Barbara H., 119
Cole, Joanna, 71

The Colors of Us (Katz), 113
The Complete Adventures of Curious George (Rey and Rey), 59–60
conversations, encouraging, 7–9
Cook, Julia, 79
Cookies (Rosenthal), 34
Cooperative Children's Book Center (CCBC), 13, 162
Cordell, Matthew, 72
Cotten, Cynthia, 150
Cottin, Menena, 118
Countdown to Kindergarten (McGhee), 76
Cousins, Lucy, 19, 74
Cullinan, Bernice, 12, 160
curiosity, books about, 57–63
Curtis, A. B., 29
Curtis, Jamie Lee, 103
Cuyler, Margery, 78

D

Dad and Me in the Morning (Lakin), 119
Dali and the Path of Dreams (Obiols), 57–58
Danzig, Dianne, 66
Davis, Katie, 75–76
Davol, Marguerite W., 114
Day Care Days (Barrett), 74
de Rico, Ul, 38
death
    parents and loved ones, 135–140
    pets, 141–145
Delval, Marie-Hélène, 155
Demas, Corinne, 143–144
Demi, 36, 38, 154
dePaola, Tomie, 138–139
deRubertis, Barbara, 86
Desser the Best Ever Cat (Smith), 141–142
Dewdney, Anna, 73–74
Diesen, Deborah, 55
Dinosaur Thunder (Bauer), 149
DiPucchio, Kelly, 22, 115
diversity, books about, 111–115
divorce, books about, 123–128
Do I Have to Go to the Hospital? (Thomas), 84
Dog Heaven (Rylant), 142
Doray, Malika, 136

Duble, Kathleen Benner, 98
Durant, Alan, 135–136
dyslexia, 107–110

E

Early Literacy Learning (website), 162
The Easter Story (Wildsmith), 155
Ehrmantraut, Brenda, 97–98
Elffers, Joost, 54–55
Emberley, Ed, 54
The Empty Pot (Demi), 36
Ernest, the Moose Who Doesn't Fit (Rayner), 27–28
Esham, Barbara, 109–110

F

Falconer, Ian, 26–27
The Fall of Freddie the Leaf (Buscaglia), 138
Fancy Nancy and the Fabulous Fashion Boutique (O'Connor), 85–86
The Fantastic Flying Books of Mr. Morris Lessmore (Joyce), 36–37
feelings, books about, 43–56
Feiffer, Kate, 69
fiction, selection criteria and, 12
Finchler, Judy, 79
Finlay, Lizzie, 86
First Day of School (Rockwell), 77
Fleming, Candace, 33–34
The Forever Dog (Cochran), 142
Fox, Mem, 40, 50, 110–111, 113
Franklin and the Thunderstorm (Bourgeois), 150
Franklin in the Dark (Bourgeois), 55
Freymann, Saxton, 54–55
friendships, books about, 17–23

G

Galda, Lee, 12
Galdone, Paul, 35–36, 47
Gesell Institute of Child Development (website), 162
Gibbons, Gail, 148–149
Gilman, Phoebe, 35
Gleeson, Libby, 92
Go Away, Big Green Monster! (Emberley), 54

God, books about, 153–156
Going to the Hospital (Parker), 84
Golding, Jacqueline, 160
Goodbye Mousie (Harris), 142
Goodnight Moon (Brown), 48
Gorbachev, Valeri, 150
Gottman, John, 43, 160
Goyangi Means Cat (McDonnell), 102
Gray, Kes, 125
The Grouchy Ladybug (Carle), 52
Grumpy Bird (Tankard), 46
guidance, book selection and, 4

H

H Is for Honor (Scillian), 99
Half a World Away (Gleeson), 92
Hall, Michael, 26
Hamanaka, Sheila, 114
Hands Are Not for Hitting (Agassi), 53
Happy Adoption Day! (McCutcheon),
    105
Hardin, Melinda, 100
Hargreaves, Roger, 48–49
Harold and the Purple Crayon
    (Johnson), 30
Harper, Jessica, 93
Harris, Robie H., 142
Harris Finds His Feet (Rayner), 31
Hart, Craig H., 160
Havill, Juanita, 78–79
Healing Stories (Golding), 160
Healy, Jane, 160
hearing issues, books about, 117–121
Heelan, Jamee Riggio, 120
Hello Baby! (Rockwell), 68
Helpguide (website), 162–163
Henkes, Kevin, 21, 49–50, 69, 75, 130
Henry Hikes to Fitchburg (Johnson), 58
Hero Dad (Hardin), 100
Hill, Susanna Leonard, 68
Hoban, Russell, 47
Homegrown House (Wong), 94
Hoopmann, Kathy, 109
Hooray for Reading Day! (Cuyler),
    78
Hooray for Summer! (Iwamura),
    151–152
Horse, Harry, 70
The Hour Glass (Japikse), 37–38

How Are You Peeling? (Freymann and
    Elffers), 54–55
How Do Dinosaurs Get Well Soon?
    (Yolen), 82–83
How Do Dinosaurs Go to School?
    (Yolen), 77
*How Do Dinosaurs Play with Their
    Friends?* (Yolen), 22
How Full Is Your Bucket? (Rath and
    Reckmeyer), 129–130
How to Be a Baby, by Me the Big Sister
    (Lloyd-Jones), 66–67
How to Be a Friend (Brown), 20
Howe, James, 44
Hurricanes! (Gibbons), 148–149

I

I Can Be Safe (Thomas), 61
I Can Share (Katz), 52
I Don't Want to Talk about It (Ransom),
    124
I Hate English (Levine), 31–32
I Like Where I Am (Harper), 93
I Love My New Toy! (Willems), 21
I Love You Like Crazy Cakes (Lewis), 103
I Miss You (Thomas), 138
I Remember Miss Perry (Brisson), 137
I Repeat, Don't Cheat! (Cuyler), 78
I Want Your Moo (Weiner and
    Neimark), 28
I Wish I Were a Butterfly (Howe), 44
I Wished for You (Richmond), 104–105
Ian's Walk (Lears), 109
If Beaver Has a Fever (Ketteman), 81–82
If You're Happy and You Know It
    (Kubler), 29
If You're Happy and You Know It
    (Warhola), 29
Ikeda, Daisaku, 31
illness, books about, 81–84
illustrations, selection criteria, 12
I'm Adopted (Rotner and Kelly), 104
The I'm Not Scared Book (Parr), 54
I'm Sorry (McBratney), 18
I'm the Best (Cousins), 19
Images of God for Young Children
    (Delval), 155
The Impossible Patriotism Project
    (Skeers), 97

The Invisible String (Karst), 37
Iris Has a Virus (Alda), 82
It's Ok to Be Different (Parr), 112
Iwamura, Kazuo, 151–152

J
Jacobs, Julie, 70
Jamaica and the Substitute Teacher
(Havill), 78–79
Japikse, Carl, 37–38
Jasper's Day (Parker), 143
Jin Woo (Bunting), 102
Johnny Appleseed (Shepherd), 59
Johnson, Crockett, 30
Johnson, D. B., 58
Johnson, Mo, 82
Johnston, Tony, 137
Joyce, William, 36–37
Julius the Baby of the World (Henkes),
69
The Junkyard Wonders (Polacco), 108
Just Kidding (Ludwig), 131
Just One Bite (Schaefer), 60

K
Kajikawa, Kimiko, 40
Karst, Patrice, 37
Kasza, Keiko, 101–102
Katz, Alan, 46–47
Katz, Karen, 52–54, 113
Keep Your Ear on the Ball (Petrillo),
118–119
Keisha Ann Can! (Kirk), 76
Kelly, Christie Watts, 71
Kelly, Sheila M., 104, 113
Kerley, Barbara, 112
Ketteman, Helen, 81–82
KidsHealth (website), 163
Kindergarten Rocks! (Davis), 75–76
King Midas (Demi), 38
Kirk, Daniel, 76
Knots on a Counting Rope (Martin and
Archambault), 118
Knuffle Bunny (Willems), 44
Koller, Jackie French, 45
Kostecki-Shaw, Jenny Sue, 20
Kotzwinkle, William, 27
Krishnaswami, Uma, 137
Kubler, Annie, 29

Kushner, Karen, 154
Kushner, Lawrence, 154

L
Lachner, Dorothea, 44
Lakin, Patricia, 119
Larson, Kirby, 148
The Last Puppy (Asch), 39
Leaf, Munro, 41
learning disabilities, books about,
107–110
Lears, Laurie, 109
The Leprechaun in the Basement
(Tucker), 88
Lester, Helen, 27
Levine, Ellen, 31–32
Levins, Sandra, 125–126
library visits, 4
life lessons, books about, 33–41
Lindsey, Kathleen D., 86–87
The Lion and the Mouse (Pinkney), 40
Listening Time (Verdick), 53
Literature and the Child (Galda,
Cullinan and Sipe), 12
The Little Chapel That Stood (Curtis),
29
Little Croc's Purse (Finlay), 86
The Little Engine That Could (Piper), 28
Little Hoot (Rosenthal), 47
Little Miss Sunshine (Hargreaves), 48
Little Rabbit's New Baby (Horse), 70
The Little Red Hen (Galdone), 35–36
Litwin, Eric, 25–26
Living with Mom and Living with Dad
(Walsh), 123–124
Llama Llama Misses Mama (Dewdney),
73–74
Lloyd-Jones, Sally, 66–67
Lola Reads to Leo (McQuinn), 66
Loth, Sebastian, 144–145
Love, Lizzie (McElroy), 98
Lovell, Patty, 132
Ludwig, Trudy, 131

M
Mackintosh, David, 23, 77
MacLachlan, Patricia, 117–118
The Magic Hat (Fox), 50
Maier, Inger, 51

Maisy Goes to Preschool (Cousins), 74
Mama and Daddy Bear's Divorce (Spelman), 124–125
A Mama for Owen (Bauer), 148
Marshall Armstrong Is New to Our School (Mackintosh), 23, 77
Martin, Bill Jr., 118
Martin, Teresa, 92
Martin, Whitney, 92
Maryland Healthy Beginnings (website), 163
Masurel, Claire, 127
Max's Castle (Banks), 60
McBratney, Sam, 17–18
McBrier, Page, 89–90
McCain, Becky Ray, 131
McCutcheon, John, 105
McDermott, Gerald, 154–155
McDonnell, Christine, 102
The McElderry Book of Aesop's Fables (Morpurgo), 36
McElroy, Lisa Tucker, 98
McGeorge, Constance W., 92
McGhee, Alison, 76
McQuinn, Anna, 66
Meiners, Cheri J., 32, 61–62
military families, books about, 95–100
Miller, Margaret, 49
Millman, Isaac, 120–121
Milway, Katie Smith, 90
Miss Bindergarten Gets Ready for Kindergarten (Slate), 76
Miss Malarkey Leaves No Reader Behind (Finchler and O'Malley), 79
mobility issues, books about, 117–121
Mollel, Tololwa M., 88–89
Mom and Dad Glue (Gray), 125
Mommy Far, Mommy Near (Peacock), 104
money, books about, 85–90
The Monster That Grew Small (Grant), 35
Montanari, Donata, 114
Moore-Mallinos, Jennifer, 103–104
Morpurgo, Michael, 36
Morris, Ann, 112–113
Mortensen, Denise Dowling, 151

Moses Goes to School (Millman), 120–121
A Mother for Choco (Kasza), 101–102
mother nature, books about, 147–152
Mouse Was Mad (Urban), 51–52
moving, books about, 91–94
Moving (Parker), 93
Mr. Happy (Hargreaves), 48–49
Mr. Tanen's Tie Trouble (Cocca-Leffler), 87–88
Mrs. Biddlebox (Smith), 45
Mrs. Gorski, I Think I Have the Wiggle Fidgets (Esham), 109–110
Ms. McCaw Learns to Draw (Zemach), 110
Murkoff, Heidi, 71
Murray, Glenn, 27
Muth, Jon J., 19, 155–156
My Big Brother (Cohen), 99
My Buddy (Osofsky), 119
My Dad's a Hero (Christiansen and Armstrong), 99–100
My Friend Has Autism (Tourville), 108–109
My Heart Is a Magic House, 70
My Heart Will Not Sit Down (Rockliff), 89
My Mom's Wedding (Bunting), 127
My Nose, Your Nose (Walsh), 114–115
My Parents are Divorced (Cochran), 125
My Preschool (Rockwell), 74–75
My Red Balloon (Bunting), 96
My Rows and Piles of Coins (Mollel), 88–89
My Shining Star (Wells), 160
My Very Own Room (Pérez), 89

N

Nana Upstairs and Nana Downstairs (dePaola), 138–139
Neimark, Jill, 28
Neo Leo (Barretta), 59
Nethery, Mary, 148
new baby, books about, 66–72
The New Baby at Your House (Cole), 71
Newman, Lesléa, 143
Night Catch (Ehrmantraut), 97–98
No Biting! (Katz), 53–54
No Such Thing (Koller), 45

Noah's Garden (Johnson), 82
Noble, Trinka Hakes, 87, 133
Nobody Knew What to Do (McCain), 131
nonfiction selection criteria, 12
Norman, Geoffrey, 97
Not a Box (Portis), 30–31
Not Everyone Is Nice (Alimonti and Tedesco), 62
Not Yet, Rose (Hill), 68
Now and Ben (Barretta), 58–59
Now We Have a Baby (Rock), 70

O

Obiols, Anna, 57–58
O'Conner, Jane, 85–86
Odd Boy Out (Brown), 58
Ohio Thunder (Mortensen), 151
Old Turtle (Wood), 153–154
Oliver at the Window (Shreeve), 127
Olivia (Falconer), 26–27
O'Malley, Kevin, 79
On Noah's Ark (Brett), 156
On the Day His Daddy Left (Adams and Adams), 126
Once upon a Dragon (Pendziwol), 61
One Hen (Milway), 90
One More Wednesday (Doray), 136
One (Otoshi), 130
One World, One Day (Kerley), 112
O'Neill, Alexis, 131–132
opportunity, creating, 5
The Orange Shoes (Noble), 87, 133
Otoshi, Kathryn, 130
Owen (Henkes), 49, 75

P

Parenteau, Shirley, 18
parents, loss of, 135–140
Parker, Marjorie Blain, 143
Parker, Vic, 84, 93
Parr, Todd, 54, 103, 112
PBS Parents (website), 163
Peacock, Carol Antoinette, 104
Pecan Pie Baby (Woodson), 69–70
Pelton, Mindy L., 97
Pendziwol, Jean E., 61
A Penguin Story (Portis), 60–61
Pérez, Amada Irma, 89

Perfect Piggies! A Book! A Song! A Celebration! (Boynton), 26
Perfect Square (Hall), 26
Pete the Cat (Litwin), 25–26
Petrillo, Genevieve, 118–119
pets, loss of, 141–145
physical illness, books about, 81–84
picture books, criteria for, 11–13
Picture This, 12–13
Pilot Mom (Duble), 98
Pinkney, Jerry, 40
Pinkney, Sandra L., 115
Piper, Watty, 28
A Place Where Hurricanes Happen (Watson), 147–148
Plant a Kiss (Rosenthal), 38–39
Plourde, Lynn, 139
Poindexter Makes a Friend (Twohy), 20–21
Polacco, Patricia, 107–108
Portis, Antoinette, 30–31, 60–61
Portnoy, Avra, 138
Potter, Beatrix, 11, 48, 61
The Pout-Pout Fish (Diesen), 55
The Princess and the Moon (Ikeda), 31

Q

The Quiet Book (Underwood), 32

R

Raatma, Lucia, 62
Rain Play (Cotten), 150
The Rainbow Goblins (de Rico), 38
Raising an Emotionally Intelligent Child (Gottman), 43, 160
Rania, Queen of Jordan, 22, 115
Ransom, Jeanie Franz, 124
Rath, Tom, 129–130
Rayner, Catherine, 27–28, 31
The Read-Aloud Handbook (Trelease), 160
Read-Alouds with Young Children (Campbell), 160
Read to Me (Cullinan), 160
reading
    developing a love of, 3–5
    talking with kids, 7–9
Reading Rockets (website), 163
Ready At Five (website), 163–164

The Recess Queen (O'Neill), 131–132
Reckmeyer, Mary, 129–130
Red, White, and Blue Good-bye (Tomp), 99
Remembering Crystal (Loth), 144–145
Remembering Grandpa (Krishnaswami), 137
resiliency, books about, 25–32
resources
    books, 159–160
    websites, 161–164
Rey, Margret and H. A., 59–60
Richmond, Marianne, 104–105
Robb, Diane Burton, 108
Robberecht, Thierry, 22–23, 67, 127–128
Robinson, Cindy, 40–41
Rock, Brock, and the Savings Shock (Bair), 88
Rock, Lois, 70
Rockliff, Mara, 89
Rockwell, Anne, 74–75, 77
Rockwell, Lizzy, 68
Rogers, Fred, 144
role models, 4
Rosenberry, Vera, 83
Rosenthal, Amy Krouse, 34, 38–39, 46–47
Rotner, Shelley, 104, 113
Russo, Marisabina, 20
Rylant, Cynthia, 142

S

Safety at the Swimming Pool (Raatma), 62
Same, Same, but Different (Kostecki-Shaw), 20
Sam's New Friend (Robberecht), 22–23, 127–128
The Sandwich Swap (Rania, Queen of Jordan), 22, 115
Sauer, Tammi, 51
Saying Goodbye to Daddy (Vigna), 136–137
Saying Goodbye to Lulu (Demas), 143–144
Scaredy Squirrel (Watt), 45
Schaefer, Lola M., 37, 60, 120
Schiller, Pam, 160
Schmitz, Tamara, 126

school days, books about, 73–79
School Library Journal, 13
Scillian, Devin, 99
Scotton, Rob, 74
Sears, Martha, 71
Sears, William, 71
Sendak, Maurice, 50
Seven Skills for School Success (Schiller), 160
Shades of Black (Pinkney), 115
Shades of People (Rotner and Kelly), 113
Shaw, Hannah, 132
Shea, Bob, 30
Sheila Rae, the Brave (Henkes), 49–50
Sheldon, Annette, 68–69
Shepherd, Jodie, 39
Shields, Gillian, 67–68
Shipton, Jonathan, 66
Shirley, Debra, 121
Show Me a Story! (Wiesner), 12
Shreeve, Elizabeth, 127
Shy Charles (Wells), 49
A Sick Day for Amos McGee (Stead), 19–20, 83
Siegel, Daniel, 160
Sipe, Lawrence, 12
Skeers, Linda, 97
Slate, Joseph, 76
Smith, Linda, 45
Smith, Maggie, 141–142
Smith, Peter K., 160
Smoky Night (Bunting), 63
Sneaky Weasel (Shaw), 132
Some Kids are Deaf (Schaefer), 120
Something from Nothing (Gilman), 35
Sometimes We Were Brave (Brisson), 96
Spalding, Andrea, 136
Spelman, Cornelia Maude, 56, 124–125
Spinelli, Eileen, 96
spirituality, books about, 153–156
Splat the Cat (Scotton), 74
Spoon (Rosenthal), 46
Squish Rabbit (Battersby), 22
Stalling (Katz), 46–47
Stand Tall, Molly Lou Melon (Lovell), 132
Standing on My Own Two Feet (Schmitz), 126
Stars Above Us (Norman), 97

Stead, Philip C., 19–20, 83
Stevens, Janet, 30
Stevenson, Robert Louis, 34, 81
Stop Picking on Me (Thomas), 130–131
The Story of Ferdinand (Leaf), 41
Surviving Deployment (website), 164
Susan Laughs (Willis), 120
Sweet, Melissa, 59
Sweet Moon Baby (Clark), 102–103
Sweet Potato Pie (Lindsey), 86–87

T
Tacky the Penguin (Lester), 27
Tafuri, Nancy, 151
A Tale of Peter Rabbit (Potter), 11
The Tale of Peter Rabbit (Potter), 48, 61
Tankard, Jeremy, 46
Tedesco, Ann, 62
Tell Me Again and the Night I Was Born
    (Curtis), 103
Ten, Nine, Eight (Bang), 46
Ten Little Fingers and Ten Little Toes
    (Fox), 111–112
The Tenth Good Thing about Barney
    (Viorst), 143
Testing Miss Malarkey (Finchler), 79
Thank You, Grandpa (Plourde), 139
Thank You, Mr. Falker (Polacco),
    107–108
That Summer (Johnston), 137
There's Going to Be a Baby
    (Burningham), 67
This Is the Sunflower (Schaefer), 37
Thomas, Pat, 61, 84, 130–131, 138
Three Little Kittens (Galdone), 47
Through Grandpa's Eyes (MacLachlan),
    117–118
Thunder Cake (Polacco), 55–56
Tom Goes to Kindergarten (Wild), 75
Tomp, Sarah Wones, 99
Tornadoes! (Gibbons), 149
The Tortoise and the Hare (Stevens), 30
Touchpoints Birth to Three (Brazelton
    and Sparrow), 159
Touchpoints Three to Six (Brazelton),
    159
Tourville, Amanda Doering, 108–109
Treasure Island (Stevenson), 81
Trelease, Jim, 160

Try and Stick with It (Meiners), 32
Tsunami! (Kajikawa), 40
Tucker, Kathy, 88
Two Bobbies (Larson and Nethery), 148
Two Homes (Masurel), 127
Twohy, Mike, 20–21

U
Underwood, Deborah, 32
Urban, Linda, 51–52

V
Verdick, Elizabeth, 53
A Very Big Bunny (Russo), 20
Vigna, Judith, 136–137
Viorst, Judith, 143
visual issues, books about, 117–121

W
Waiting for Baby (Ziefert), 72
Walsh, Melanie, 114–115, 123–124
Walter, the Farting Dog (Kotzwinkle and
    Murray), 27
Walter Warthog's Wonderful Wagon
    (deRubertis), 86
Warhola, James, 29
Was It the Chocolate Pudding? (Levins),
    125–126
Watson, Renée, 147–148
Watt, Mélanie, 45
We Are Adopted (Moore-Mallinos),
    103–104
We Are Best Friends (Aliki), 93–94
We Belong Together (Parr), 103
Weiner, Marcella Bakur, 28
Wells, Rosemary, 49, 77–78, 160
Wemberly Worried (Henkes), 50, 75
What Baby Needs (Sears, Sears, and
    Kelly), 71
*What to Expect When the New Baby
    Comes Home* (Murkoff), 71
What to Read When (Allyn), 159
When a Pet Dies (Rogers), 144
When Dad's at Sea (Pelton), 97
*When Fuzzy Was Afraid of Losing His
    Mother* (Maier), 51
When I Care about Others (Spelman), 56
*When Lizzy Was Afraid of Trying New
    Things* (Maier), 51

When the World Was Waiting for You
   (Shields), 67–68
When Vera Was Sick (Rosenberry), 83
Where Do People Go When They Die?
   (Portnoy), 138
Where Is God? (Kushner and Kushner),
   154
Where Is Grandpa? (Barron), 139
Where the Wild Things Are (Sendak), 50
Where's My Teddy? (Alborough), 54
While You Are Away (Spinelli), 96
Whoever You Are (Fox), 113
The Whole-Brain Child (Siegel), 160
Wiesner, David, 12
Wild, Margaret, 75
Wildsmith, Brian, 155
Wilfrid Gordon McDonald Partridge
   (Fox), 40
Willems, Mo, 21, 44, 139–140, 144

Willis, Jeanne, 120
Wilson, Karma, 52
Wong, Janet S., 94
Wood, Douglas, 153–154
Woodson, Jacqueline, 69–70

Y
Yes We Can! (McBratney), 17–18
Yoko Learns to Read (Wells), 77–78
Yolen, Jane, 22, 77, 82–83
You Will Be My Friend! (Brown), 18–19
Your Child's Growing Mind (Healy), 160

Z
Zemach, Kaethe, 110
Zen Shorts (Muth), 155–156
Zen Ties (Muth), 19
Zero to Three (website), 164
Ziefert, Harriet, 72